THE VENERABLE
BEDE

OUTSTANDING CHRISTIAN
THINKERS SERIES

Series Editor: Brian Davies OP, Professor of Philosophy at
Fordham University, New York.

Cappadocians Anthony Meredith SJ	**Hans Urs von Balthasar** John O'Donnell SJ
Augustine Mary T. Clark RSCJ	**Teresa of Avila** Archbishop Rowan Williams
Catherine of Siena Giuliana Cavallini OP	**Bultmann** David Fergusson
Kierkegaard Julia Watkin	**Karl Barth** John Webster
Lonergan Frederick Rowe SJ	**Aquinas** Brian Davies OP
Reinhold Neibuhr Kenneth Durkin	**Paul Tillich** John Heywood Thomas
Venerable Bede Benedicta Ward SLG	**Karl Rahner** William V. Dych SJ
Apostolic Fathers Simon Tugwell OP	**Anselm** G. R. Evans
Denys the Areopagite Andrew Louth	

THE VENERABLE BEDE

Benedicta Ward SLG

continuum
LONDON • NEW YORK

Continuum

The Tower Building, 11 York Road, London SE1 7NX
370 Lexington Avenue, New York, NY, 10017-6550

First published 1990, reissued with additions 1998

Re-issued 2002

British Library Cataloguing-in-Publication Data
A catalogue record for this book is available from the British Library.

ISBN 0 8264 5785 1

Typeset by YHT Ltd, London
Printed and bound in Great Britain by
Biddles Ltd, Guildford and King's Lynn

Contents

Editorial Foreword

St Anselm of Canterbury (1033–1109) once described himself as someone with faith seeking understanding. In words addressed to God he says 'I long to understand in some degree thy truth, which my heart believes and loves. For I do not seek to understand that I may believe, but believe in order to understand.'

This is what Christians have always inevitably said, either explicitly or implicitly. Christianity rests on faith, but it also has content. It teaches and proclaims a distinctive and challenging view of reality. It naturally encourages reflection. It is something to think about; something about which one might even have second thoughts.

But what have the greatest Christian thinkers said? And is it worth saying? Does it engage with modern problems? Does it provide us with a vision to live by? Does it make sense? Can it be preached? Is it believable?

The Outstanding Christian Thinkers series is offered to readers with questions like these in mind. It aims to provide clear, authoritative and critical accounts of outstanding Christian writers from New Testament times to the present. It ranges across the full spectrum of Christian thought to include Catholic and Protestant thinkers, thinkers from East and West, thinkers ancient, mediaeval and modern.

The series draws on the best scholarship currently available, so it will interest all with a professional concern for the history of Christian ideas. But contributors also write for general readers who have little or no previous knowledge of the subjects to be dealt with. Its volumes should therefore prove helpful at a popular as well as an academic level. For the most part they are devoted to a single thinker, but occasionally the subject is a movement or school of thought.

Brian Davies OP

Acknowledgements

In presenting a book which covers all Bede's works I am conscious that I am, to use his own phrase, 'following in the footsteps of the Fathers' and drawing together the work of many illustrious predecessors to whom I owe an inexpressible debt of gratitude. I am also grateful to colleagues and pupils over the last twenty years for much stimulating discussion about Bede and Anglo-Saxon England. I would like to thank my sisters at the Convent of the Incarnation, Oxford, and the brothers of the monastery of the Holy Cross, Chevetogne, for time and space to complete the work, and especially Sister Christine SLG who prepared the index.

This new edition contains a fuller bibliography and some additions to the text on the cult of Bede.

Benedicta Ward SLG
Oxford 1997

1

Bede and his times

There is no brilliance in Bede but much steady clarity; no overtones and undertones, no subtle intuition, no lightning flash of genius. He lives and writes in the noon-day sun. . . . Simple, sane, loyal, trusting, warm-hearted, serious with that ready sense of pathos which has always been a mark of English literature . . . falsehood and vanity of any kind were quite foreign to him . . . a good man who, as he himself said, could live without shame and die without fear.[1]

This sensitive portrait of one great historian by another is remarkable for the sense of intimate acquaintance and even friendship which it conveys. It is an interior knowledge of a man rather than knowledge about him and is characteristic of those who read and ponder Bede's writings. The first editor of Bede's *Ecclesiastical History of the English People* broke through his customary reserve with a similar remark:

It is no light privilege to have been for so long a time in constant communion with one of the saintliest characters ever produced by the church of this island.[2]

This sense of immediate knowledge and appreciation as of a contemporary is the more remarkable for the small amount of fact that is known about Bede. He left no personal account of himself and no contemporary celebrated him with either a hagiography or a biography; he appears in no chronicles of the times, nor did he take any part in the government of the abbey or the church of which he was a member all his life; in no instance can his mark be detected in official documents of any kind. And yet it is possible to know Bede more intimately than any other man of his time, whether in his relationship to Christ and his view of salvation or in his opinions on sex and his admiration for the fashion in beards.

BEDE'S LIFE

It is through his writings that Bede is known in this face to face encounter and these illuminate the sparse 'facts' of his life which he himself summarized at the end of his *Ecclesiastical History of the English People*, following an example set by Gregory of Tours:[3]

> I, Bede, servant of God and priest of the monastery of St Peter and St Paul which is at Wearmouth and Jarrow, have, with the help of God and to the best of my ability, put together this account of the Church of Britain and of the English people in particular, gleaned either from ancient documents or from tradition or from my own knowledge. I was born in the territory of this monastery. When I was seven years of age I was, by the care of kinsmen, put into the charge of the reverend abbot Benedict and then of Ceolfrith, to be educated. From then on I have spent all my life in this monastery, applying myself entirely to the study of the Scriptures; and amid the observance of the discipline of the Rule and the daily task of singing in the church, it has always been my delight to learn or to teach or to write. At the age of nineteen I was ordained deacon and at the age of thirty priest, both times through the ministration of the reverend Bishop John on the direction of Abbot Ceolfrith. From the time I became priest until the fifty-ninth year of my life I have made it my business, for my own benefit and that of my brothers, to make brief extracts from the works of the venerable fathers on the holy Scriptures, or to add notes of my own to clarify their sense and interpretation.[4]

This summary of a life is what a monk should write; what else of importance was there to say, apart from the great moments of reception into the monastery, ordination as a cleric, the ordinary round of daily life until death? Based on the ideals of monasticism it may be, but that is not to say that it is anything other than a true reflection of Bede's life also. The passage is of a piece with Bede's other writings, and in them all there is a quality of concentrated attention to and unaffected delight in his life as a monk. There was, however, a different strand of colour woven into the plain cloth of Bede's monastic life: he was a writer and a well-known one at that; he followed his brief summary of his life with a long and carefully exact list of his own writings.

It is possible to fill in some details about the circumstances of Bede's life within the framework that he himself set out. From the date he gave for the completion of *The Ecclesiastical History of the English People* it seems that he was born in 673.[5] His name was an unusual one though it was also that of a monk at Lindisfarne. He identified himself with the 'English people' (*gens anglorum*) in his treatise *De Temporum Ratione*, when he gave a description of the names the English gave to the months of the year:

It does not seem to be appropriate that when giving an account of the way other races arrange the year, I should be silent about the observances of my own race.

Almost certainly his kinsmen had been both English and Christian, since they offered the boy to a monastery, presumably after his parents' death. Bede wanted to be identified as English but only as an English Christian and he ends his account of the English months with:

Thanks be to you, good Jesus, for turning us from these vanities and granting us to offer you the sacrifice of praise.[6]

Bede never mentioned his own family elsewhere in his writings, a freedom from ties of kin which, though certainly part of monastic ideology, might also suggest that his birth was not noble, since he was always ready to mention the noble rank of others, even though it was to say 'noble by birth but more noble by grace'. 'Home' for Bede was his monastery and when at the age of fifty-nine he wrote about his life, he gave as the place of his birth 'the lands of the monastery', although at that time the monastery had not existed.

Bede's love for the abbots of the twin Northumbrian monasteries at Wearmouth and Jarrow is patent in every page of his *History of the Abbots* and it is probable that this affection was based not only on his place as a child of the cloister at Wearmouth under its founder Benedict Biscop (628–689), but also on his survival through an outbreak of plague in the foundation made from Wearmouth at Jarrow, together with its first abbot, Ceolfrith (d. 716). In the

3

anonymous *Life of Ceolfrith* there is an account of the terrible plague of 686 which struck the north of England with particular violence and reduced the number of monks at the new and fragile foundation at Jarrow to Abbot Ceolfrith, and a boy of the monastic school; others survived but none who were part of the monastic choir:

> In the monastery over which Ceolfrith presided, all who could read or preach or recite the antiphons were swept away, except the abbot himself and one little lad nourished and taught by him, who is now a priest of the same monastery and both by word of mouth and by writing commends to all who wish to know them the abbot's worthy deeds. And the abbot, sad at heart because of this visitation, ordained that, contrary to their former rite, they should, except at vespers and matins, recite their psalms without antiphons. And when this had been done with many tears and lamentations on his part for the space of a week, he could not bear it any longer, but decreed that the psalms with their antiphons should be restored to their order according to the regular course; and by means of himself and the aforesaid boy, he carried out with no little labour that which he had decreed, until he could either train them himself or procure from elsewhere men able to take part in the divine service.[7]

This description of a 'little lad nourished and taught by him' as well as 'one who by writing commends to those who wish to know them the abbot's worthy deeds' fits Bede very well. Moreover, if this was not Bede, then what happened to him during the total destruction caused in his monastery by the plague? If this was indeed Bede, such a traumatic event surely accentuated both his isolation and his dependence upon Ceolfrith, as upon a father and sole surviving plank in a stormy sea. When Ceolfrith later finally left Jarrow to go the Rome to end his days among the saints of the early Church, Bede seems to have experienced a crisis in his life. He wrote two accounts of the departure; one, the official account in the *History of the Abbots*, is controlled and edifying and entirely impersonal.[8] The second, which was written first, in the days immediately after the event, is in the letter accompanying his *Commentary on Samuel*. It is very revealing, both about Bede's attachment to Ceolfrith and the emotional impact of this separation on Bede, and also about the absorption in his writing which made him oblivious to this event until it was happening:

Having completed the third book of the *Commentary on Samuel*, I thought I would rest awhile and after recovering in that way my delight in study and writing, proceed to take in hand the fourth. But that rest—if sudden anguish of mind can be called rest—has turned out much longer than I had intended, owing to the sudden change of circumstances brought about by the departure of my most reverend abbot, who after long devotion to the care of his monastery, suddenly determined to go to Rome and to breathe his last breath amid the localities sanctified by the bodies of the blessed apostles and martyrs of Christ, thus causing no little consternation to those committed to his charge, the greater because it was unexpected. He removed the ancient Moses, appointed Joshua to the leadership and ordained Eleazar to the priesthood in the place of the father Aaron. So in the place of the aged Ceolfrith who was hastening to the threshold of the apostles, he ordained the young Hwaetberht who by his love and his zeal for purity had long since won for himself the name of Eusebius and after the brethren had elected him, he confirmed the appointment by his blessing brought by your ministry, dearest bishop. And now with the return of quieter times, I have again leisure and delight for searching out the wondrous things of the Scriptures carefully and with my whole soul.[9]

While this passage illustrates Bede's attachment to Ceolfrith, it also provides insight into Bede as a writer and monk. Absorbed in the steady round of his life in the monastery, he found the departure of Ceolfrith 'sudden' and 'unexpected', whereas in the *Life of Ceolfrith* it is clear that the journey was an open secret and had been planned for some time.[10] Above all it underlines Bede's priorities: the limitations of his life were of choice as much as of rule. Other monks travelled widely, besides Ceolfrith. This letter itself, for instance, was addressed to Bishop Acca of Hexham (700–732), another much-travelled monastic friend. Bede was shocked by the departure of Ceolfrith but he showed no inclination to follow him; his concern was to regain the freedom of mind necessary for study in the monastery. Nor did he ever travel widely. Benedict Biscop, his first abbot, was renowned for his journeys abroad and Bede must have often heard of the wonders of the Mediterranean world as well as seen the marvels brought back from it, but he never went there himself. With all his interest in the archives of the papacy, it was the priest Nothelm who checked them for him.[11] His only visits

5

of which there is any record were local and austerely connected with his writing: he went to Lindisfarne once at least in connection with his *Life of St Cuthbert*;[12] he visited York at the end of his life to talk with his former pupil Egbert about contemporary church affairs;[13] and he visited the monastery of a certain Abbot Wihtred, where he discussed some of the intricacies of computation.[14] In a homily on Benedict Biscop, he talked about 'we who remain within the monastery walls', with gratitude that this was possible;

> He [Benedict Biscop] worked so zealously that we are freed from the need to labour in this way; he journeyed so many times to places across the sea, that we, abounding in all the resources of spiritual knowledge, can as a result be at peace within the cloisters of the monastery, with secure freedom to serve Christ.[15]

This 'peace' was Bede's choice even though it was not all gain, and at the end of his *Commentary on the Song of Songs* he wrote about the dangers of misunderstanding for those who, like himself, were not personally in touch with the wider world of Christian culture, isolated in the distant island of Britain.[16] For Bede, unlike many of his Northumbrian contemporaries, the centre of the world of the mind was Rome; but his body remained in his cell, above all among books and parchments. This 'single eye' of the monk-writer, so clearly a child of the cloister, may well have been the reason for his lack of involvement in any of the practical affairs of his monastery.

BEDE THE PUPIL

Bede's concentration on the life of the mind depended upon three things besides his own abilities: his teachers, the books available to him, and contact with others, teachers, colleagues and pupils, with whom he could share his thoughts, whether in word or in writing. His teachers must have included the great men of Wearmouth when he first went there, and he described Benedict Biscop, Ceolfrith and Sigfrid, another abbot of Wearmouth (d. 688), as, in their different ways, men of deep learning who had earned his respect and gratitude.[17] He must have learned, whether directly or indirectly, about the world outside the cloister from his first abbot, the much travelled ex-thane of King Oswiu, who founded the two monasteries and received Bede as a child.[18] Sigfrid, who died when Bede was fifteen, he described as 'amply learned in knowledge of the Scriptures'.[19] His affection for Ceolfrith may well have gone along with instruction by him as a child, especially in Latin, that basis of all Bede's scholarship. He says in a letter to Plegwine, a monk of Hexham, that he was instructed early in chronological studies, and perhaps this branch of learning also was learned from Ceolfrith. In 680 just after Bede came to the abbey, another great teacher arrived: John the archchanter of St Peter's in Rome came with Benedict Biscop in order to teach chant at Wearmouth. It appeared later that John was also a Vatican spy[20] reporting back to Rome on the doctrinal position which he found in Britain, that island from which had come the monk Pelagius, whose views on grace had been countered by Augustine of Hippo in the fourth century. But for Bede, John was the teacher whom he was to follow as master of the school at Jarrow. He mentions also Trumbert, an Irish monk of Lastingham, as one of his teachers:

> ... a certain brother named Trumbert ... one of them that taught me in the Scriptures and was brought up in Chad's monastery and government.[21]

Chad, bishop of the Mercians (d. 672), was described by Bede with affection and veneration.[22] He had been trained in the Scriptures in Ireland and had founded the monastery of Lastingham, where Trumbert was educated. This fact may have contributed to Bede's admiration for the Irish and his anxiety about their views on the dating of Easter. Lastly, Bede was ordained both deacon and priest by the saintly John of Beverley, whose miracles he recorded;[23] perhaps this bishop, who had been trained by both Theodore of Canterbury (d. 690) and Hilda of Whitby (614–680), exercised some influence also on Bede.

What did they teach him? Latin certainly, and later Bede learned Greek, perhaps under the influence of the Greek Theodore of Tarsus (archbishop of Canterbury 688–690) and his learned companion the African Hadrian, of whom Bede wrote admiringly 'Both of them were extremely learned in sacred and secular literature'; he added 'some of their students still survive who know Latin and Greek as well as their native tongue'. [24] Their school in Kent seems to have influenced the education Bede received at Jarrow; indeed, his own writings correspond to the list he gives of subjects taught at Canterbury: 'the books of holy Scripture, the arts of metre, astronomy, and ecclesiastical computation'.[25] Both Albinus, the successor of Hadrian as abbot of the monastery of St Peter and St Paul (later known as St Augustine's), whom Bede knew well, and a certain Tobias are mentioned by Bede as pupils in that school of learning and therefore competent in Greek. One book at least survives which may have been brought to England by Archbishop Theodore and may have been used by Bede: it is a copy of the Acts of the Apostles, written in double columns with the Greek text on one side and a translation into Latin on the other.[26] The curriculum at Wearmouth and Jarrow was perhaps close to that outlined by Bede's contemporary Aldhelm of Malmesbury (639–709), who said that when he studied at Canterbury under Theodore and Hadrian, in addition to excellent instruction in Latin and Greek, he learned Roman law, methods of combining chant and verse and other poetic arts, mathematical calculation, and the zodiac.

BEDE'S LIBRARY

The necessary tools for instruction by such masters were books; they were not only the source but also the aim of such learning. The books Bede used came to him at first through Benedict Biscop, whose journeys to the Mediterranean gave his monasteries a library of unique value, filled above all with copies of the text of the Bible and commentaries on many of its books. Bede says Ceolfrith doubled the number of volumes the library contained. There is no library list surviving from either Wearmouth or Jarrow and the volumes are long since dispersed; it is only possible to discover what books Bede read through his own writings. Most of the books Bede used were in his own monastery, while others he no doubt borrowed from the libraries which were being built up in Canterbury, Hexham and York. He knew a variety of texts of the Bible, the Old Latin versions, Jerome's Vulgate, the Septuagint Greek, and he frequently discussed the textual problems they presented. It is possible, indeed probable, that his knowledge in this area was utilized for the production of three great Bibles, one of which, the *Codex Amiatinus*, still provides one of the best early Latin texts of the Scriptures. Through the Office, he was well acquainted with the old Roman psalter, which had remained in liturgical use long after Jerome's revised version of the other books of the Bible had become popular.

Along with the Bible, Bede read commentaries on the Scriptures. He was the first to name Augustine, Ambrose, Jerome and Gregory as the four great Fathers of the Church and their commentaries provided his main source for biblical exegesis. The twin libraries at Wearmouth-Jarrow probably contained a large number of early grammatical works, some books of Isidore's *Etymologies*, at least parts of Pliny's *Natural History* and many works of the early Christian poets, all of whom Bede used in teaching.

The histories at his disposal included Eusebius's *Ecclesiastical History* in the Latin version by Rufinus, several chronicles, including Jerome's translation of the *Chronicle* by Eusebius, Jerome's *De Viris Illustribus*, and works by Josephus, Orosius, Gildas, Cassiodorus, Marcellinus and Gregory of Tours. For Biblical commentaries, he had to hand many works by Augustine, Ambrose, Jerome and Gregory the Great, and others by Origen, Cassiodorus, Hilary, Cyprian and Victorinus.[27]

For books specifically about monastic affairs, it seems that Bede knew the Rule of St Benedict, though how far the daily conduct of his life was regulated by this text is by no means clear. There are several passages in his works which show a deep appreciation of the Rule of St Benedict, but it would be anachronistic to suppose that the monastery at Jarrow in any sense 'followed' St Benedict's Rule: the life of the brothers was lived in obedience to Christ through the guidance of the abbot, and while Benedict Biscop knew the Rule of St Benedict, he drew upon many other ancient rules as well as personal observation and advice gained during his travels for the organization of the life in his monasteries, all being modified and adapted to existing conditions in Northumbria and among new Christians. The Rule of St Benedict was for Bede both more and less than has sometimes been claimed: it was not a 'rule' in the sense of exclusive regulations for a code of behaviour, but it was, perhaps, a 'rule' in the sense of a greatly esteemed source of wisdom providing a norm for reference.[28]

As a monk, Bede's life contained another formative influence, that of the daily round of liturgical prayer, which shaped his mind from his first days in the monastery as a child of seven until his death. The Scriptures, and especially the Psalms, have always formed the basis of the texts of the monastic Office in the Western Church, whether in the order given in the Rule of St Benedict or not. Bede met with his brothers seven times in the day and once in the night to recite with them the psalter and to hear read or sung other parts of the Scriptures; it was the focus to which all his learning was directed. He was known for his 'delight to sing' and a story told later by Alcuin illustrates his care for attendance in choir:

It is said that our master and your patron, the blessed Bede, said, 'I know that angels visit the canonical hours and the meetings of the brethren. What if they should not find me there among them? Will they not say, where is Bede? Why does he not come to the devotions prescribed for the brethren?'[29]

The monk Cuthbert, a pupil of Bede, recorded that when Bede was dying the texts that came naturally to his mind were the antiphons from the Office, among them the antiphon for the Magnificat for vespers of the feast of the Ascension, which he could not sing without tears.

As one of the priests of the monastery, a deep devotion to the Eucharist also marked Bede's life. In his writings, he constantly urged ordained priests to be better pastors and more devout celebrants, while the laity, he felt, should come more frequently to communion. A passage from his commentary on the gospel of Luke expressed clearly his serious and devout frame of mind:

> Whenever we enter the church and draw near to the heavenly mysteries, we ought to approach with all humility and fear, both because of the presence of the angelic powers and out of the reverence due to the sacred oblation; for as the angels are said to have stood by the Lord's body when it lay in the tomb, so we must believe that they are present in the celebration of the mysteries of his most sacred body at the time of consecration.[30]

The framework of Bede's life was liturgical, and it was a liturgy both respected and loved, having a profound influence on his thought and writing. Such an influence came to him through books as well as by word of mouth from his teachers. As a natural part of life, Bede had therefore an example of Latin style always before him, forming not only his mind but also his Latinity.

Bibles, commentaries and liturgical books had first reached Jarrow from Europe and especially from Rome, but by Bede's time the books from abroad were not the only volumes in the libraries of the Anglo-Saxons. The Mediterranean books had begun to be copied, in a hand which was both legible and distinctive. Bede himself took part in the copying of manuscripts, at times acting as his own amanuensis, as well as urging his pupils and fellow-monks to accuracy in copying texts. The great books of Wearmouth–Jarrow came from a scriptorium where books were not ornaments but tools. Elsewhere, big picture-books like the Lindisfarne Gospels and the Book of Kells presented vivid and lively images on their pages, continuing a means of communication already familiar in carvings to a nation without a written language; but at Jarrow they were scholars and Roman scholars at that. Such books as survive from that scriptorium have few if any pictures or ornamentation; their beauty lies in a clear, well-formed hand. Like Bede's works, they were meant to be used rather than wondered at.

BEDE'S COLLEAGUES

Bede's interests may have been concentrated on learning and writing, but he was not a solitary, alone in his cell with his books. He was a member of a vigorous young community, with teachers, friends and pupils. Within the monastery, Bede's contemporaries may well have died during the plague which he survived with Ceolfrith but as Jarrow revived he had both younger colleagues and pupils. He offered one of his early works to his 'dearest son and fellow deacon, Cuthbert', and his *De Temporum Ratione* was addressed to Hwaetberht, a young Saxon who was given the nickname of 'Eusebius', an able and energetic monk of Jarrow who visited Rome and eventually succeeded Ceolfrith in 716, as Bede's 'most beloved abbot'. In Bede's *Life of St Cuthbert* there are references to other monks of Jarrow whom Bede knew well: Sigfrid, who had been a young monk at Melrose in the time of St Cuthbert, ended his days at Jarrow; a priest, Ingald, who told Bede about a miracle of Cuthbert, was a monk of Wearmouth, and a priest-monk of Jarrow told him about another miracle in which the hermit Fergild had been cured by touching a relic of Cuthbert. In the *Ecclesiastical History* Bede mentioned the names of other monks of his monastery, as men whom he talked with about the past: Cynemund, for instance, told him about a miracle of Aidan which he in turn had heard about from Bishop Utta. There was also Eadgisl the monk who told Bede about a judgement which befell the abbey of Coldingham, and it was from another monk of Jarrow that Bede heard about the Irish visionary Fursa. With all the names he mentioned, Bede was always careful to add, if appropriate, their status as 'priest' as well as monk, often in the phrase, 'my fellow priest-monk', a small indication of the pride and pleasure he felt in belonging to the ranks of the clergy.

Outside Jarrow, Bede had many monastic friends with whom he corresponded about subjects of mutual interest in the world of learning and letters. There was, for instance, a monk of Hexham, his 'most beloved brother' Plegwine, who wrote to tell Bede that he had been accused of heresy by the priest David in the presence of Bishop Wilfrid.[31] Bede wrote also to his 'dearest brother in Christ', the monk Helmwald, to wish him well as he set out on a pilgrimage. He knew and trusted Albinus, abbot of St Augustine's in Canterbury, claiming that he was 'the principal authority' and 'helper' of his last great historical work.

Twice at least Bede visited friends in other monasteries. Wihtred, a priest and perhaps an abbot, had welcomed Bede to his abbey to discuss chronology and Bede wrote to thank him. Bede also visited Lindisfarne, for consultation about his revision of his account of their greatest saint. He knew the abbot Eadfrid, the creator of the Lindisfarne Gospels, and talked at length with the old monk Herefrid who had known Cuthbert intimately and was prepared to tell Bede in detail about Cuthbert's death, information he seems to have withheld from the monk of his own house who wrote a previous *Life* of the saint. At Lindisfarne, Bede knew also Baldhelm, Cynemund and Guthfrid the sacrist, who all supplied him readily with intimate and personal reminiscences of Cuthbert, a fact which suggests a man easy to talk to and trust. At the end of his life, he also visited his former pupil Egbert in York, and was planning to do so again, when prevented by his last illness.

The *Ecclesiastical History* contains much information about nuns, but Bede himself seems to have had little personal contact with any. He may have corresponded with the abbesses of Ely and of Whitby about the information he included in the *Ecclesiastical History* concerning their houses, and he made a *Commentary on the Canticle of Habakkuk*, another text used in the Office, for his 'dearest sister in Christ', a nun and perhaps an abbess, possibly at one of the convents he praised for their learning, such as Whitby or Ely.

Among the clergy in general Bede had many friends and correspondents. He wrote often to Acca, bishop of Hexham, a man of wide learning with an excellent library, who shared Bede's love of biblical exegesis and was the recipient of many of his commentaries as well as providing much information for Bede's historical writings. Bede called him 'the lord most beloved in Christ', 'the most dear and beloved of all the bishops who dwell in these lands', 'the lord most blessed and ever to be revered with deepest love'. Acca is mentioned in connection with nine of Bede's commentaries as well as his *Libri Retractationis* on Acts and a poem on the Final

12

Judgement.[32] There was also 'my most beloved lord in Christ', John, a priest to whom Bede sent his metrical *Life of St Cuthbert* as light reading for his journey to Rome. There was an anonymous 'friend from Britain', presumably a cleric, who questioned the future Pope Gregory II in Rome sometime before 716 and sent back to Bede information which he mentioned in his work on Acts.

Another man of learning with interests overlapping with those of Bede was Nothelm, a priest of the church of London, a friend of Albinus and later archbishop of Canterbury. He put thirty questions to Bede about certain points in the Book of Kings which he thought required elucidation and it was Nothelm who was chosen by Albinus to convey information about Kent to Bede in Northumbria. Bede later trusted his scholarship so far as to accept his transcriptions of the Roman archives about the mission of Augustine to Kent. In the Preface to the *Ecclesiastical History* Bede also mentioned Daniel, bishop of Winchester and Cynebert, bishop of Lindsey, as well as the abbot Esi as correspondents providing information for his work. Wilfrid of York met Bede at least once and they were on good enough terms for Bede to question him about a most intimate matter concerning the virginity of Queen Aethelthryth through two marriages, in which Wilfrid had been her spiritual adviser. Other correspondents may have sent Bede information from coastal districts about the tides, which he used in his book *De Natura Rerum*.

A man devoted to learning through books and letters, Bede also culled much information from visitors to his monastery. Jarrow was by no means an out of the way place; it was a rich, well-endowed abbey, international in its contacts, lying at the centre of England, between the highly cultured kingdom of Dalriada to the north, the learned though eccentric Irish to the west and the English kingdoms to the south, with good sea contact to Gaul and the Mediterranean. In this flourishing kingdom, the monasteries Bede knew best were closely connected with the royal house. A king had given money for the foundations of Wearmouth and Jarrow, their first abbot had been a thane of the king and Bede dedicated his last work to King Ceonwulf, sending him a first draft for his approval. The house at Jarrow was lavishly enriched with cut stone, glass and frescoes as well as books and charters. Many noblemen visited the monastery and gave it gifts. Some of the noble visitors found their way to the cell of Bede where they were welcomed not for their rank but for their information.

BEDE'S AUDIENCE

Visitors told Bede much and it may be that he also spoke to them for their benefit. He was deeply and personally concerned always with the communication of the richness of the Christian faith to all, literate and unlearned, poor and rich alike. He included among his activities sermons to the brothers, whether in chapter or during the liturgy, and perhaps he also preached to the people who visited the monastery. A story told about him in his old age indicates his reputation for preaching to all who came, and incidentally reveals the uncouth side of some of his young brothers:

> After Bede had devoted himself for a long time to the study of Holy Scripture, in his old age his eyes became dim and he could not see. Some mockers said to him, 'Bede, behold, the people are gathered together waiting to hear the word of God, arise and preach to them'. And he, thirsting for the salvation of souls, went up and preached, thinking that there were people there, whereas there was no-one but the mockers. And as he concluded his sermon, saying, 'This may God deign to grant us, the Father, the Son, and the Holy Ghost', the blessed angels in the air responded saying, 'Amen, very venerable Bede'.[33]

Bede and his friends, with their care for learning, prayer and preaching, were perhaps the exception rather than the rule among Anglo-Saxon monks; monasteries were not all filled with the devout, and Bede's master, Ceolfrith, also had experience of these 'mockers': he once left the monastery because of the unruly noblemen in it and the *History of the Abbots* praises him for being 'remarkably strenuous in restraining evil doers'.[34]

Bede was determined to communicate what he knew at every level of society, but his first responsibility was for the men and boys of his own monastery. For them he produced the tools for Christian learning, conveying the skills of the ancient world as far as possible with reference to the Bible, the Fathers and the early Christian poets. Like Gregory the Great, he was suspicious of the classics. He described secular studies as 'the husks with which the swine were fed, full of sterile sweetness' and exclaimed over Jerome's love for Cicero, 'often even noble masters of the church, victors in great struggles, have fallen into sin by reading the books of the gentiles'. Of his pupils a few are known by name, and none of them ever equalled their master: the monk Cuthbert who later became abbot of Jarrow wrote an account of Bede's death which had occurred while he was himself Bede's pupil and he mentions in it the boy Wilberht who took down the last words of Bede as he translated part of the Gospel of St John into English. Bede's last visit was to Egbert, a former pupil, with whom he talked about the state of the Church in England in 734 when Egbert had become bishop of York.

Bede was a man of wide and international culture, and he was always more than the schoolmaster of a monastery on the edge of the civilized world. But just as his first care was for his own pupils at Jarrow, so he was also concerned for his own race. He was the first to coin the phrase *gens Anglorum*, 'the English nation', and he longed for his race to become a people of God, not by abandoning their identity but by discovering it. This was not the ideology of a distant scholar but a practical programme. For instance, in the most fundamental matter of a written language, Bede wanted his countrymen to know Latin and enter the wider world of Latin literature connected with the text of the Bible but he recognized that it might not be possible. He mentions more than once that he found the English unready to study Latin assiduously and when in the last year of his life he wrote to Egbert, he had realized that many of them would never learn it at all. He therefore recommended a minimum at least of translation into the newly-created written language of English and he said that he himself had already prepared such translations of the Lord's Prayer and the Creed. It is significant that his last work was a translation of a gospel into English. Though himself possessed of a great thirst for learning so that he knew Latin perfectly, Greek well and even Hebrew as far as he could, Bede was no pedant; it was the content of the Gospel he wanted to convey, not the externals, and if others could not share his enthusiasm for the ancient languages, he was prepared to use Anglo-Saxon to give them the essentials of Christianity. The monk Cuthbert in his letter on Bede's death described him as an expert in Anglo-Saxon poetry and quoted an English song which Bede sang when dying. Although Bede ran easily through the entrancing fields of the learning of late antiquity, he did not forget that he lived in a more rugged world among newly-converted barbarians.

Bede's Northumbria was a world full of energy and life. When Bede was given as a boy to Wearmouth, barely a hundred years had passed since Augustine had been sent from Rome by Gregory the Great to convert the Anglo-Saxons. Augustine (d. 604) had established Christianity in Kent by the baptism of the Saxon pagan king, Aethelberht; forty years later, the Greek Theodore had come to

England as archbishop of Canterbury, bringing a world of new learning. Christianity had reached the North through Paulinus (d. 644), chaplain to Aethelburgh, Aethelberht's daughter, who married Edwin, king of Northumbria. But the North also became Christian through another kind of missionary activity, that of the Irish. Many Anglo-Saxons had fled for political reasons to Ireland, and were baptized while in exile there; others went there to contact the Irish tradition of Christian learning; and in 635 the monk Aidan joined the Christian king Oswald in Northumbria in a concerted programme of conversion. Benedict Biscop had been a thane of one of Oswald's successors, Oswiu of Northumbria, and Oswiu's successor Ecgfrith gave him the lands upon which Bede's monastery was founded.

Bede therefore grew up in a monastery closely connected with the vigorous new Christian culture of England, with its complex association of kings and churchmen and its contacts with both Ireland, Gaul and the Mediterranean. He was an integral part of it and his writings more than any others gave it coherence. Bede's account of the people and events of his own land was set within the perspective of the whole of Christian history, stretching back to the first days of the faith in Palestine. His exegetical works gave to his contemporaries the riches of the learning of the early Church. The first Roman missionaries had brought with them relics of the apostles; Bede saw England as a land based on the teaching of those apostles. His works ensured that the early history of Christianity in England would be remembered; by recording the past, he made sure that the present would reach the future.

When Bede ended his last great work, the *Ecclesiastical History of the English People*, in 731, he quoted two psalms from the past of Israel, relating them to his own times in which his race looked to the future of 'his perpetual kingdom':

> This is the state of Britain at the present time, about 285 years after the coming of the English to Britain. Let the earth rejoice in his perpetual kingdom and let Britain rejoice in his faith and let the multitude of the isles be glad and give thanks at the remembrance of his holiness.[35]

The fact that such a vision of a peaceful and Christian England was even desirable was to a large extent the work of Bede. In an age of conquest and warfare, in a society built on wealth and violence this was a remarkable achievement. But still more remarkable than Bede's place within that new and violent world was his stature as the most learned man of his age and one of the Doctors of the Universal Church.

Notes

1 David Knowles, *Saints and Scholars: Twenty Five Medieval Portraits* (Cambridge, 1962), ch. 2, 'Bede the Venerable', pp. 17–18.

2 HE(P) I, Editor's Preface, p. v.

3 Gregory of Tours, *History of the Franks*, trans. Lewis Thorpe (Harmondsworth, 1974), X.31, pp. 602–4.

4 HE, V.24, pp. 567–71.

5 Cf. HE(P) I, note 1, p. xi, for discussion of the dates of Bede's life. *Usque ad annum aetatis meae LVIIII* has been understood to mean either 'until' or 'in' the fifty-ninth year of his age, giving either 672 or 673.

6 DTR, xv, pp. 329–32.

7 *Life of Ceolfrith*, trans. D. S. Boutflower (London, 1912), 14, p. 65.

8 HA (Farmer), 16, 17, pp. 202–3.

9 *Samuel* IV, p. 212; trans. C. Plummer in HE(P) I, pp. xv–xvi.

10 *Life of Ceolfrith*, 21–23, pp. 70–80.

11 HE, Preface, p. 5.

12 VSC, Prologue, p 145.

13 *Letter to Egbert* (Whitelock), pp. 35–45.

14 *Letter to Wihtred*, ed. C. W. Jones, CCSL CXXIIIC (Turnhout, 1980), pp. 617–26.

15 *Homilies* I, no. 13, p. 94.

16 *Song of Songs*, p. 180.

17 *Homilies* I, 13, p. 93.

18 Cf. HA (Farmer), 1–7, pp. 185–92.

19 Ibid., 10, p. 195.

20 Ibid., 6, pp. 190–1 and HE, IV.18, pp. 389–91.

21 HE, IV.3, p. 343.

22 For Bede's respect for Chad cf. HE, IV.3, pp. 337–47.

23 Ibid., V.2, pp. 457–73.

24 Ibid., IV.2, p. 335.

25 Ibid., IV.3, p. 337.

26 *Codex Laudianus Graecus* (MS Bodley 35).

27 For an analysis of books available to Bede cf. M. L. W. Laistner, 'The library of the Venerable Bede' in BLTW, pp. 237-66.

28 For discussion of the role of the Rule of St Benedict at Jarrow see H. Mayr-Harting, *The Venerable Bede, the Rule of St Benedict and Social Class* (Jarrow Lecture, 1976); P. Wormald, 'Bede and Benedict Biscop' in *Famulus Christi*, pp. 141-70.

29 Quoted by C. Plummer, HE(P) I, p. xii. Latin text in *Councils and Ecclesiastical Documents relating to Great Britain and Ireland*, ed. A. W. Haddan and W. Stubbs, vol. 3, pp. 470-1. There is little direct evidence about the liturgical practices at Jarrow, but see Cabrol and Leclercq, *Dictionnaire d'archéologie chrétienne et de liturgie*. XV. i, col. 1166, XV.ii, cols 2436-7 (under *'Ordines romani'*).

30 *Homilies* II, iv, p. 121.

31 *Letter to Plegwine*, ed. C. W. Jones: CCSL CCXIIIC, pp. 635-42.

32 Acca, bishop of Hexham. For an admirable summary of Bede's relationship with Acca and others see D. Whitelock, 'Bede and his teachers and friends' in *Famulus Christi*, pp. 19-40.

33 Quoted by C. Plummer, HE(P) I, p. xlviii.

34 HA (Farmer), p. 202.

35 HE, V.23, p. 561.

2

Bede the teacher

'It was always my delight to learn and to teach':[1] at the end of his life, Bede saw himself as having been not only a scholar but equally a teacher. Himself taught by kindly and wise men at Wearmouth and Jarrow, in his turn he instructed the newcomers to the monastery. The fact that his didactic works proved to be of lasting importance and continuing influence on European thought should not obscure the immensely practical slant of Bede's teaching, whether to the boys and men of the cloister or to interested readers in other places.

As in any age and place, the energies of the majority of people in Anglo-Saxon England were absorbed by the simple facts of living; they had neither time nor inclination for speculation. But then as now there were those whose curiosity stretched beyond the immediate moment and whose circumstances permitted them to allow their interests to range over extraordinarily wide horizons. In the classroom at Jarrow, Bede was charged with the education of some of these among the newcomers, and from his own speculations he offered them an astonishing and varied equipment with which to view their world and their existence in it. Bede, in the excitement of his own discoveries, presented to his pupils and later wrote into books for other more distant learners, not only the central realities of the spiritual world of the resurrection as seen in the pages of the Bible, but also the structure of the natural world, seen in the same text as created by God, and man's place within it. But before opening up the natural history of the world, the calculation of time, the framework of the universe, the Anglo-Saxon novices had to be taught more fundamental things: reading, writing and arithmetic, and these were essential not optional. In order to take part in the daily Offices, the monk needed to be able to sing and to know by heart a great deal of Scripture. He could learn it by repetition and if all he needed to do was join in choral singing and chant, he might do well enough without more learning. But the chief readers and singers had to know how to read and proclaim alone. Moreover, anyone destined for the priesthood would need to be able to read and study and learn by reading in order to preach and give counsel as well as administer the sacraments. Bede's first task was, therefore, to teach the novices Latin: to memorize it, to read and intone it aloud and also to study through it. It was the obvious requirement for any study, as Augustine of Hippo had said in *On Christian Doctrine*, 'he will be the most expert investigator of the Holy Scriptures who has first of all read them'.[2]

LEARNING TO READ AND WRITE

How were the illiterate Anglo-Saxons, with no written language of their own, taught to read and write Latin? After the withdrawal of the Roman legions from Britain the decline of schools for Latin learning had begun. It did not revive there until the seventh century, and then in an entirely new mode. The first missionaries had been occupied in the task of preaching and baptizing, but Theodore of Canterbury with Hadrian had begun the process of formal education for monks and clergy forty years before Bede's birth. To expand and solidify this method of education, which based learning on the study of the Bible, was the work of Bede. His pupils were monks who had a definite purpose in mind in studying at all and their learning is best understood as part of their work in the conversion of England rather than as essential to their monastic life. Study was not an obvious necessity for monks. Earlier Christian ascetic traditions had seen learning for a monk as suspect, leading to vanity and useless speculation. In the atmosphere of Roman Egypt, Palestine or Italy, a tradition of literacy could form a positive impediment to the calling of the monk. The majority of monks in fourth-century Egypt were illiterate and those among them who were learned had to be alert to see that such learning proved neither divisive nor a temptation to pride: 'An old man said, "reading books is good but possessing nothing is more than all" '.[3] In such an atmosphere, the highly cultured Arsenius and the scholarly Evagrius found special need of solitude and silence to achieve this evangelical freedom about learning; both Jerome and Palladius found it impossible. But the illiterate Egyptians were part of a Church in which learning was well-established and widespread; the question for such monks was one of priorities and of balance.

The Anglo-Saxons, on the contrary, had no tradition of book-learning around them; and it was essential that some at least should be able to read the Gospel. Where there were no centuries of Christian tradition, artificial means were necessary to create it and the monks, with stability of place, were in the best position to provide a centre for such literacy. In Kent, Augustine was an example of the educated monk-missionary and in Northumbria there was a model of learned monasticism in the Irish monk-scholars. Moreover, contact with monasteries in other places in the barbarian West indicated the need for book-learning, in order to be in touch at first hand with the one book that was fundamental to the Christian life, the Bible. Unlike the early Christian ascetics, many of the monks in England as elsewhere were also priests, and their lives therefore contained a second strand; they were not only part of the solitary tradition which had taken Columba to the island of Iona in the sixth century, but of the tradition of men of the Scriptures which had caused Cuthbert to study with Boisil at the abbey of Melrose in the seventh. Such attention to reading was never literacy for its own sake; it was necessary to acquire direct contact with the text of the Gospel in order to learn how to give it to others. The text Bede used to describe Cuthbert's reading with Boisil was a motto for the whole enterprise of monastic scholarship: 'the faith that works by love' (Galatians 5:6).[4] For the Anglo-Saxon monks in the eighth century, there was no native literate culture; they needed the basic tools, not the vanities, of learning before they could safely enter in at the strait gate. In other words, they needed first of all Latin grammar, but in relation to the new book, the Bible, and that only.

It was Bede who converted the secular learning of the ancient world into a new mode, suitable for monks and priests, and as far as possible he taught from new sources. Bede himself was essentially a man of the Bible and whenever he could, he taught Latin through the Bible, usually the elegant Latin of Jerome's Vulgate, not through the classics, and often advised caution in using classical authors as guides to Latinity, even when there was no option:

Every teacher who is careful to rule his subjects with effective authority and to conduct himself without offence believes he must be helped sometimes by the arguments and opinions of the Gentiles.[5]

But in such a case, there was great need for care:

With much more caution must the rose be plucked from among sharp thorns than the lily from soft leaves; much more securely is sound advice sought in apostolic than in Platonic pages.[6]

Bede distrusted the content of the works of pagan writers and, however necessary it might be to use the Latin grammarians, he warned his pupils of their danger and provided alternatives. It was not that he was ignorant of earlier grammatical texts; when he wrote his treatises on grammar and on poetic form, he used the grammarians of the late Roman empire—Donatus, Charisius, Diomedes, Pompeius, Sergius, Audax, Victorinus, Mallius, Theodorus, Servius, Agroecius, Caper, Dositheus—all of whom must therefore have been available in some form in England in the eighth century. But as with all he read, Bede absorbed the content and reshaped it for the new needs of his times. His earliest surviving work, *De Orthographia*, is a notebook, with words grouped under letters of the alphabet, with brief warnings about difficulties in spelling, a few grammatical notes about certain forms, sometimes alternative meanings: of use, surely, mostly to the one who made it.[7] Some examples in it are from the classics, but others from the Fathers; it is not a distinguished work, but it is something basic that remains of the class books of Bede's Jarrow, where he taught the young to read Latin.

Bede's more extensive teaching on grammar is contained in 'a book on metre' to which he added 'a small book on figures of speech or tropes, that is, converting the figures and modes of speech with which the Holy Scriptures are adorned', and in these he used quotations from the Bible and from the Christian poets to replace pagan authors. Bede's treatises explaining metre formed a group and include teaching about grammar. They were constructed by Bede's favourite method of beginning with the smallest elements and proceeding in ever widening circles. He began with the letters of the Latin alphabet, the basic material for verse as for prose, and added to the twenty-one Latin letters five more, giving them Scriptural authority.[8] He then proceeded to discuss what could be made from the letters, and from such simple beginnings he led his pupils through an exacting course on metre, explaining all the classical forms clearly. In *De Schematis et Tropis* he summarized the forms of speech and gave examples of them from the Scriptures and the Christian poets, including in chapter 12 a useful introduction, which he expanded in other places, on the different meanings of the scriptures, historical, mystical, tropological and anagogical.[9] In this he was not simply conveying the learning of the ancient world to the Anglo-Saxons; the material was organized and simplified with skill. Bede's mastery of the poetic material available to him was complete and in his treatises on verse he provided an indispensable tract for later ages, not only encapsulating the teaching of the ancient world but doing at least one new thing by treating the new rhythm of isosyllabic stress as a distinct poetic form.[10]

The ability to read Latin put the Anglo-Saxons in touch with the Christian past and the world of Christian learning in the present; it gave permanance and continuity. Before long, it was this skill of forming letters that enabled them to create a written form for their own language also. But first they needed to learn the existing written language of Latin. With this they could communicate beyond the present moment into the future as well as to other places. Space and time were given new dimensions and what most of all widened their horizons was the ability to write. On wax tablets, on clay, on slates, and then on parchment they learned to form letters and to write Latin prose as good as their teacher could make it. In order to have books at all, it was necessary to take the examples Benedict Biscop had brought to this isolated place and copy them; beyond that lay composition of new things in Latin. Though not the master of the scriptorium, Bede was charged with instructing the novices in written forms, sentences, verbs, nouns, grammatical construction, so that they could copy with intelligence and perhaps write for themselves later.

Both master and pupils approached letters and language with keen interest. For Bede, language was the way in which man spoke about the Word of God and all his works show a continual interest in words and languages. Grammatical explanations of names in the Bible are inserted into the commentaries on the Scriptures and in the *Ecclesiastical History* there are frequent notes about languages. For his pupils, this skill of writing was not limited in its application to monastic or even church affairs: kings wanted written texts, partly for the usefulness of a permanent record of law, partly for the simple glory of possessing the new skill of writing in one's court, and partly for the possibility of recording the glory of the past which had been so greatly valued in the sagas and heroic songs of the Anglo-Saxon tradition. Scribes were welcome in the households of secular as well as ecclesiastical dignitaries.

Nor was Bede concerned only with prose. He was himself a poet and intent on introducing his pupils to Latin poetic forms. As well as his treatises on metre, he composed a large amount of Latin verse in both elegiac and hexameter metre. His verse life of Cuthbert of Lindisfarne was a thousand hexameters long, constructed according to the rules of classical poetry, and his long poem in praise of Queen Aethelthryth was written in equally competent elegiacs. The poem *On the Day of Judgement*,[11] if it is in fact by Bede, shows again his mastery of the hexameter form. For his first Biblical commentary he wrote a rather mannered verse preface, 'On Blessed John and His Apocalypse', ending with the elegant and genial lines:

> If these my scanty morsels please thy taste
> Give praise to God, who reigns above the skies;
> Or else, accept a friendly heart's intent,
> And, armed with pumice, this my verse erase.[12]

Perhaps the fact that he was writing for one of his brothers at Jarrow, Hwaetberht, himself a versifier, caused Bede to use this mode of easy address. More often, his use of verse was practical rather than decorative. Verse was memorable, and it was also useful in that it could be declaimed and heard, as well as adding also beauty and dignity to reading and singing.

The world of the Anglo-Saxons through Bede and his contemporaries became filled with books and the excitement and fascination the Anglo-Saxons found with letters was phenomenal. It was reflected in the intricate and lovely decoration they wove into their books; it was reflected also in their puns, word-games and riddles, always popular as entertainment orally, now even more exciting in writing. The answers to riddles would often have to do with writing itself as in this Latin riddle of Hwaetberht of Jarrow, to which the answer is 'a pen':

> In kind simple am I nor gain from anywhere wisdom,
> But now each man of wisdom always traces my footsteps.
> Habiting now broad earth, high heaven I formerly wandered;
> Though I am seen to be white, I leave black traces behind me.[13]

The same fascination is apparent in a more complex riddle by his contemporary Aldhelm of Malmesbury, to which the answer is 'a wax writing-tablet':

> Of honey laden bees I first was born;
> But in the forest grew my outer coat;
> My tough backs came from shoes. An iron point
> In artful windings cuts a fair design,
> And leaves long, twisted furrows like a plough.
> From heaven unto that field is borne the seed
> Or nourishment, which brings forth generous sheaves
> A thousandfold. Alas, that such a crop
> A holy harvest falls before grim war.[14]

Perhaps impelled most of all by delight in such word-games, the Anglo-Saxons very soon had created a written language of their own; they used it for prose, as in the *Anglo-Saxon Chronicle*, but also for poetry. Anglo-Saxon puns and riddles were made with the same lively interest in word-play as in Latin. For example, on the same theme of books, there is this riddle in Anglo-Saxon, which begins with the preparation of parchment:

> A life-thief stole my worldly strength,
> Ripped off flesh and left me skin,
> Dipped me in water and drew me out,
> Stretched me bare in the tight sun . . .

It goes on to deal with the quill, the ink, the binding and the use of a book.[15]

But poetry for Bede was a serious matter; he wrote no riddles or puns but looked with concerned interest into the classic metres of poetry, and their use by the early Christian poets such as Prudentius, Venantius Fortunatus and Ambrose. Perhaps the response of this monastery-bred boy to poetry was an inheritance from his own race with its high poetic oral tradition which led him instinctively to look into the poetic traditions of the Latin world, but more consciously he was attracted towards poetic forms by discovering them in the Bible and in the Fathers: he regarded Job and King David as fellow poets, and was encouraged to think that even the mother of God had sung a poem in her Magnificat. Moreover, he was well aware that the Divine Office contained hymns especially for the greatest of feasts, a use praised by Fathers such as Augustine

25

and Ambrose. The hymn-writers Fortunatus, Prudentius, Paulinus, Sedulius and Avitus were all Fathers of the Church, and their works could therefore be used and their example followed with the greatest assurance.

Poetry for Bede was a craft, a discipline, which must be learned and mastered, but it was infinitely more; it was inspired by God. In the *Ecclesiastical History*, Bede gave a detailed account of the Anglo-Saxon poet Caedmon, whose poems provided the earliest written Anglo-Saxon verse. The story is a description of poetic inspiration, of the gift of poetry which was then directed by the disciplines of poetic form. In a dream the cowherd Caedmon, a frustrated poet unable to join in the evenings of singing to the harp with his fellow servants in the monastic lands at Whitby, dreamed that *quidam*, not an angel or a saint, but 'someone', stood by him and told him to sing, choosing for him the theme of all great poetry: 'Sing about the beginning of created things'. Waking, he remembered his verses, and freed from his mental block, learned from the great men, the scholars and bards of Whitby, how to shape and communicate his gift, turning the scriptures into fine verses in his own language.[16] It is an account to be read alongside the treatises of Bede on poetry, so that the rules of the ancient world can be seen at work among the simplest of the new Christians, not as a rediscovered technique but as the vehicle for the expression of true poetic insight.

Bede's love of poetry lasted all his life and in his account of Bede's death, the monk Cuthbert related that in addition to chanting the Latin psalms in his last days he also used English: 'in our own language—for he was familiar with English poetry—speaking of the soul's dread departure from the body he would repeat:

> Facing that enforced journey, no man can be
> More prudent than he has good call to be.
> If he consider, before his going hence,
> What for his spirit of good hap or of evil
> After his day of death shall be determined.'[17]

Whether or not Bede composed the verse he sang, his affection for and knowledge of Anglo-Saxon verse is amply demonstrated.

LEARNING ABOUT NUMBERS

As well as these basic skills, the monks needed to know how to count and with this went the whole range of subjects which were covered by the word *computus*. The treatises *De Temporibus* and the longer *De Temporum Ratione*, Bede's computistical works, displaced all rivals in the schools of the West. His choices about time fundamentally determined the calculations of time which still govern our own existence. No handbooks were as skilful or as popular as Bede's, and the fact that they survive in such fragmentary form before the ninth century points to the hard classroom use that they received. Later, glosses on the texts and commentaries adapted Bede's work to a wide range of situations for centuries. As with the works on grammar, Bede began with what is smallest and most basic, in this case counting numbers. In the *De Temporum Ratione*, the first chapter is Bede's version of the ancient skill of finger-counting: 'On Counting and Talking with the Fingers'. This, as he says, could provide a secret sign-language for the boys, since each number signified also a letter; the example he gives is well adapted to the interests of schoolboys:

> If your friend is placed among enemies and you want to warn him to be careful, make the finger signs for three, one, twenty, nineteen, five, and for one, seven and five, which will mean *'Caute age'* ('Be careful').[18]

The games of the schoolboys with numbers were merely a diversion. Numbers were to Bede and indeed to all learned men of the ancient world, a complete and complex language, and about every number several things could be said, opening the doors to other realities in a way similar to the language of letters. By filling the minds of his pupils not only with words but also with numbers, Bede gave them a place in time as well as in space. And at the heart of this interest lay the central fact of the Christian religion: the moment of the death and resurrection of Christ, which each year had become the focus for the entry of new Christians into that 'new life' by baptism. The Chronicle which forms part of *De Temporum Ratione* has as its first entry the year AD 1:

> In the forty-second year of Caesar Augustus, twenty-seven years from the death of Cleopatra and Antony when Egypt became a province, the third year after the 193rd Olympiad, 752 years from the foundation of the city, that is in that year

whence by the ordaining of God Caesar imposed a most sure and true peace, Jesus Christ the son of God consecrated the sixth age of the world by his coming.

This gave popularity to calculations of time centred on the birth of Christ, but it is the entry for the year AD 33 that contains the most momentous statement: 'in the eighteenth year of the Emperor Tiberius, God redeemed the world by his passion'.[19]

The calculations of the day upon which this pivotal fact was to be celebrated each year varied; it was not a fixed date like that of the Nativity, and where there is a possibility of variation there is also the possibility of dispute and disunity.[20] For the Christians in England as much as elsewhere, the whole of time was seen to hinge upon that one moment of a new reality, a new creation, the breaking through of heaven into earth, and disunity about it had the deepest theological implications. It is no accident that a central chapter of the *Ecclesiastical History* is concerned with the resolution of a contemporary dispute between the Roman missionaries and those from Ireland about the date of Easter. It was not just a desire for uniformity or an exercise in authority that caused Bede to think and write so earnestly about the correct dating of Easter and to spend so much ink on providing correct Easter tables, nor was his calculation a purely secular matter connected with the earth's revolutions. Here was the point where time crossed with eternity and all the symbolism of heaven and earth had to be focused to bring this into view.

There was biblical warrant for celebrating Easter near to the date of Passover; not only did the evangelists say that the crucifixion took place in connection with the feast of the Passover, but Passover itself supplied the fundamental images through which they interpreted the event: it was celebrated in the first month of the Jewish year, Nisan, in which God created the world, and it was also the celebration of the delivery of the people of God from slavery in Egypt, major themes through which Christians understood redemption as a new creation and a new Passover. The early alienation of Christians from the Jewish community in which they had lived and the increasing antagonism between Jews and Christians meant that Easter was soon not celebrated on exactly the same day as Passover but on the new holy day of Sunday; eventually it was also decided that Easter and Passover should never coincide. In his reading of the Fathers, Bede found discussion of the date of Easter on these lines, especially in the account given by Eusebius,

Bede's model for a Church historian, in his description of the Easter controversies of the first Christian centuries and their resolution by the Council of Nicaea (AD 325). But the first problems had been resolved in the first three centuries by the decision to celebrate Easter annually and on Sunday, but not on the same date as the Passover to which it had been inevitably linked; to achieve this with certainty, Easter should not be celebrated before the Passover date of 14 Nisan itself. The Quartodeciman heresy, so often referred to in discussions of the dating of Easter, was about the custom some Christians in Asia Minor had of continuing to celebrate Easter on whatever day of the week Passover fell. This was regarded as an aberration and had been disallowed by the third century; at the Council of Nicaea the decision that the date of Easter should be calculated without reference to Passover confirmed their condemnation. By the eighth century the term 'quartodecimans' had no real meaning and was used simply to suggest error; the problem before the Anglo-Saxon Church was not about this issue.

There were three points still open for discussion: firstly, it was still a question whether, if Passover fell on a Sunday, Easter could also be celebrated on that day. Secondly, a matter to be considered in determining the date of Easter was the time of the first full moon of the first month and this was found by a lunar calculation. A third factor to be considered by the Christians was the date of the vernal equinox, since from a symbolic point of view the night of the vigil of Easter had to be that after which light increased in the world, and that is a solar calculation. The linking of the light given by both sun and moon, moving as they do in different cycles in relation to the earth, demanded the expertise of a mathematician and an astronomer, as well as a biblical scholar well-versed in the Synoptic and the Johannine accounts of the Passion, and the comments of early Fathers and Councils on the subject. It involved the calculation of lunar and solar cycles of years with delicate adjustments to make them work. In the early Church the astronomical centre of Alexandria and the administrative centre of Rome had combined to issue the paschal letters, telling each year the correct date of Easter; by the eighth century, such letters were a thing of the past, astronomical calculation was unknown to the vast majority of Christians, and various tables for the determination of both moon and equinox circulated; that of Dionysius Exiguus in any case ended in 724 and needed to be continued.

What concerned the Anglo-Saxon was that the missionaries who came to them from Rome and Gaul sometimes celebrated Easter on a different Sunday from the missionaries who came to them from Iona and Ireland, sometimes a week apart, sometimes four weeks. It was a matter which could be practically inconvenient as well as theologically unedifying, involving not just the day of Easter but the Lent of forty days fast, traditionally the preparation for baptism, which preceded it, and the fifty days after, the Pentecost, which culminated in the second great moment for the baptism of new Christians. Bede's skill as an astronomer was in this issue combined with his knowledge of the Scriptures and the Fathers, to clarify and support the resolution of a matter of immediate concern to English Christians. The celebration of the Resurrection was to be in the first month of the Jewish year, the month Nisan, in which God had created the world and led the people out of Egypt. Nisan contained the annual celebration of Passover on the fourteenth night when the moon was full. It was not at all clear how this month was determined for the Jews, but for Christians this lunar month had to be determined astronomically. It was no use waiting for spring each year and then going out to look at the phase of the moon and deciding to accept the next full moon as the paschal moon. Calculations had to be made concerning the moon's phases for as many years ahead as possible, most of all because the forty days of fasting before Easter was already universally customary and its beginning had to be determined. Moreover, the problem of the calculation of Easter extended beyond itself to the whole of the Christian calendar, in which Sundays of the year were seen in relation to Easter, while the saints' days were fixed in the solar calendar's month.

There was no disagreement between Celts and Romans about the celebration of Easter in the night on the first Sunday after the full moon after the vernal equinox; rather, they disagreed about two different ways of deciding which was the first Sunday after the Easter full moon. To determine the time of the vernal equinox the revolution of earth in relation to the sun had to be calculated over a series of years, until the full cycle of years was complete and therefore repeated, and here the Celts immediately differed from the Roman party by using a different cycle of years. By the tables they were using, the equinox occurred on 25 March, while more recent calculations had taken into account certain problems in the Julian calendar and fixed the equinox on 21 March. Thus, sometimes a full moon might occur just before 25 March but after 21 March; in this case, it would not be counted as the Easter moon by the Celts, who would wait for the next lunar month, which they would then regard as the first month containing the paschal moon;

but for the Romans, the moon was full before their vernal equinox and therefore they would celebrate Easter on the next Sunday after it: a difference of four weeks would result.

Another problem arose concerning the definition of the beginning of the day. For the Celts each day began at dawn, so that if the full moon rose at any point in the night Saturday/Sunday they regarded that Sunday as 'after' the full moon and celebrated it as Easter. But for the Romans each 'day' began on the previous evening, so that if the full moon appeared after midnight Saturday/Sunday, that day was not 'after' the full moon and they would therefore wait until the next Sunday: the difference of a week resulted. Moreover it was possible to have another week's difference if Passover coincided with the Sunday after the Easter full moon, since the Celts regarded this as Easter and the Romans did not.

The matter had been resolved before Bede's time at the Council of Whitby by the decision of King Oswiu in favour of the authority of St Peter and Rome, but the dispute was not finally settled everywhere for fifty years and it was Bede who by his advocacy of the need for unity and his careful and learned discussions of the factors involved ensured that this would be the case from conviction as well as obedience in the Celtic Church in his own time as well as in the Western Church ever since.

Bede was by no means the most fierce of those who debated the Easter question, nor was he blinded by the external arithmetic involved. It was not an idolatry, and when describing the life of Aidan, while he deplored the fact that Aidan had not shared in this unifying celebration, he added,

> In his celebration of Easter he had no other thought in his heart and preached no other doctrine than we do, namely the redemption of the human race by the passion, resurrection and ascension into heaven of the one mediator between God and man, Jesus Christ (cf. 1 Timothy 2:5).[21]

Bede's interest in numbers provided him also with another language, just as absorbing as that to be discovered through letters. He used numbers as part of the symbolic understanding of the Bible and was constantly expanding the text by exploring any number mentioned to illuminate doctrine and clarify conduct. For instance, he found the deepest significance in the number eleven and when discussing the election of Matthias to make up the number of the Twelve, he wrote:

Peter was afraid that the apostles should remain in the eleventh number, for every sin is an eleventh because while it acts perversely it transgresses the precepts of the Ten Commandments. Wherefore, because no righteousness of ours is innocent, the tabernacle which contained the ark of the Lord was covered from above with eleven curtains of goats' hair (Exodus 26:7). And he completes again the number of the apostles as twelve so that by the two parts of the number 7 (3 + 4) they might preserve the grace which they preached in word with number also (3 × 4 = 12) and that those destined to preach the faith of the Holy Trinity to the quadriform world, as the Lord says, 'Go, teach all nations baptising them in the name of the Father and of the Son and of the Holy Spirit' (Acts 1:16), might also confirm the perfection of the work by the sacrament of number also.[22]

Such interpretation of numbers was usual in the commentaries of the Fathers; it presupposed not only an alertness to the significance of each number but an inbuilt concordance of Scripture in the memory, so that the numbers connected and illuminated one another. For example, the number seven, made up of either three and four, or six and one, or five and two, had any number of significances: four might be the four elements of the world, three the Trinity and seven the combination of both in the Incarnation of Christ. Twelve could signify the whole Church because 'the four-square world subsists by the faith of the Holy Trinity, for three times four are ten and two'.[23] Augustine used numerology lavishly, while Isidore wrote a special treatise on the significance of numbers in the Bible. Behind it lay a long tradition of symbolism and numbers and a determination to make every number as well as every letter of the Scriptures a way of listening to the Word of God. In Bede's works, it was neither forced nor arbitrary, and, as Charles Plummer observed,

> It often has that high degree of appropriateness and beauty which springs from a true spiritual insight into that divine order wherein all things are doubled one against another, that fair harmony of things, that wondrous sacramental concord.[24]

Numbers also gave Bede his framework for the history of the world, which he divided into six ages, with a seventh running concurrently and an eighth still to come.[25] The days of the week of Easter lay behind this in the early Church, which in turn relied on the idea of six days of creation in Genesis, ending in the seventh day of the rest of the Creator. In the Christian dispensation these were completed by an 'eighth day' which was also the first and only day of the New Creation. To the symbolism of these 'ages' Bede added the 'ages' of a man's life, seeing all history from the time of Adam's expulsion from paradise as five 'ages', corresponding to the periods of a man's life. In the sixth age, which is still in progress, Christ was incarnate; this last, old age, of the world, runs alongside the seventh age of the rest of the saints and the culmination of both is to be the eighth day of eternity.[26]

Bede was also interested in the number of years from the Creation to the end of the world and in his rearrangement in this area he differed from some of his contemporaries. Popular millenarianism had taken the phrase used in 2 Peter 3:8: 'one day is with the Lord as a thousand years and a thousand years is as one day' and interpreted it in connection with the consummation of all things to mean that each of the five ages of the world had been a thousand years long and the last age, beginning in AD 1, would also last a thousand years; thus arriving at a foreseeable Day of Judgement in the year AD 1000. Bede countered such a notion in *De Temporibus*, where he set the beginning of the sixth age at 3,952 years from Creation instead of 5,199, which destroyed the millennial calculation. In 708, when he was thirty-five and an established writer, he was told that he had been cited as a heretic on this subject before the aged Bishop Wilfrid of York. In *De Temporum Ratione* he had challenged the calculation of the last age of the world by his recalculation of the years belonging to each age, while saying, as did Augustine, that the end of the last age and the coming of Christ was known only to God: 'it is not for you to know the times and the seasons', he quoted, 'that the Father has put in his own power' (Acts 1:8). The charge of heresy distressed Bede profoundly: he wrote to a friend:

> How could I, denying Christ, be a priest of the church of Christ and with what logic could I, believing in the gospels and the epistles, disbelieve that he had become incarnate in the sixth age?

Bede was sure he was innocent, never altered his opinions, but became almost hysterically sensitive to such criticism which he regarded as both ignorant and malicious. In this case, he wrote to Plegwine, asking him to make a certain 'David' help in clearing his name:

I beseech you to forward this letter clearing me to our religious and very learned brother David, so that he can read it in the presence of our venerable lord and father Wilfrid the bishop.

The charge of heresy had come out of ignorance and, he suspected, perhaps out of drunken irresponsibility. The charge had been made, he said,

> at that table at which one is drunk with the cup. . . . I am grieved enough, as angry as is lawful and more angry than I am accustomed to be.[27]

In *De Temporum Ratione*, written seventeen years later, Bede was still angry about the same matter; as a master of his subject he was outraged, and the more so since it touched on the merits of the Greek and Hebrew versions of the Bible. It seemed to him a total misunderstanding of what he was doing; and the worst of it was, his friends had not come to his defence.

LEARNING ABOUT THE WORLD

Bede's curiosity, like that of Augustine, extended beyond written words and the art of numbers. He was interested in the natural world, as it issued from the hand of God. Much of his natural science was included, as with so many of the Fathers, in his biblical commentaries and especially, though not exclusively, in his comments on the description of the creation of the world in the first chapters of Genesis. The information inserted there overlapped with that contained in his more formal treatise, *De Natura Rerum*. It is easy to see the intense interest Bede had in created things. For instance, in his treatise on Revelation, his first essay in commenting on the Scriptures, he spent more time than he had intended discussing the jewels named as foundations of the new Jerusalem (Revelation 21:18–22). Fascinated by their appearance and the significance he discovered in these gems, he provided an extended commentary which is in fact a lapidary, in which the ancient tradition of significance in gems was turned into Christological commentary. First he described the physical appearance of various kinds of jasper, one 'green marked with flowers', another like an opaque emerald, a third 'glistening with snow and the foam of sea waves', then, collecting other scriptural references, he saw the significance of the gem as the unfading green of faith, which is filled with the sacrament of the Lord's passion by the water of baptism and is prepared by increasing merits with all the flowers of spiritual gifts.

He began his analysis of each stone with the physical description of the gem in question, then explored its significance, each bit of information from the ancient world being surrounded by passages from scripture to lead into a Christological interpretation:

By jasper therefore is shown the unfading greenness of faith, which by the water of baptism is filled with the sacrament of the Lord's passion and is prepared by growing merit for all the flowers of spiritual grace. He who has this puts vain fears to flight as the blessed Peter warns us, 'Your adversary the devil goes about as a roaring lion seeking whom he may devour, whom resist steadfast in the faith' (1 Peter 5:8) and he is able to say with the Bride, 'My beloved is white and ruddy' (Song of Songs 5:10). Therefore with good reason in Isaiah also the bulwarks of the same city are said to be fortified and adorned by this stone and structure of the wall (Isaiah 54:12).[28]

Elsewhere, Bede gave his attention to the natural phenomena of the course of the moon, the sun, the stars and the planets, which were linked with his interest in time. He was also interested in the earth itself, which he described as

made of the four elements, earth, air, fire and water, of which all things are composed and all of which move naturally towards the centre of the earth.[29]

The earth itself he described as a globe banded by five temperature zones, cold at the poles, very hot at the equator and temperate in the middle bands. That the earth was round was common knowledge in the ancient world but Bede saw it as three-dimensional:

The earth is placed in the centre of the universe not only in latitude so that it is round like a shield but rather in every direction like a ball no matter which way it is turned.[30]

It followed from this that he thought all sides of the earth could be inhabited. Other natural phenomena caught his interest from observation as well as from books. Shadow lengths could provide information about latitudes and Bede gave the calculations of latitudes which he found in Pliny with a full explanation of his system confirmed by experiment. In the *Ecclesiastical History* he commented on the northerly position of Britain:

The winter nights are also of great length, namely eighteen hours, doubtless because the sun has then departed for the region of Africa. In summer too the nights are extremely short, each consisting of six standard equinoctial fours, while in Armenia, Macedonia, Italy and other countries in the same latitude the longest day or night consists in fifteen hours and the shortest in nine.[31]

The study of the shadow thrown by a stick placed upright at noon of the day of the equinox had also been used in the ancient world, not only in relation to the heavens but also by architects and engineers; Bede's *De Natura Rerum* provided shadow lengths for each of the eight parallel bands circling the earth. He had something new to add to ancient learning about the relationship between the moon and tides, by collecting and correlating information from places such as Lindisfarne, Whithorn and the Isle of Wight. By his nineteen-year lunar table it was possible to predict the movement of tides with a high degree of accuracy, allowing for local variations. His theories were not substantially expanded until the time of Robert Grosseteste (1173–1253) and in principle they were not altered until Newton in the seventeenth century provided a new framework for thinking about the relationship of the sun, moon and earth to one another.

Bede had little previous knowledge at his disposal; the *Etymologies* of Isidore of Seville (560–663) which incorporated some of Pliny, he used at first freely, treating them as a handy encyclopaedia of miscellaneous texts. Later, Bede learned to be critical of Isidore and one of his last works was an attempt to guard his pupils against such errors as the *Etymologies* might contain; Isidore was to be used but not uncritically. Bede's interest in features of the natural world expanded naturally from his reading of the Scriptures, especially from the account of the creation of the world in Genesis; his reasonable and methodical approach to the material before him enabled him to assemble such learning as he could, pass it on in a clear form and add to it where possible.

TEACHING THE UNLETTERED

Not everyone wanted to know. Intellectual curiosity is not a universal gift and its implementation depends on the amount of time and energy spent on extending it. Bede found the average Anglo-Saxon less than ready to read, write and calculate, especially in Latin.

Owine, a thane of Queen Aethelthryth, who decided to become a monk, walked from East Anglia to the abbey of Lastingham carrying an axe and an adze, signifying his refusal to enter the schoolroom, and he never did:

> When they [the monks] were engaged in reading inside the house he used to work outside at whatever was necessary.[32]

Many of the converted soldiers would have found the classroom both undignified and puzzling; Benedict Biscop himself may have learned to read but accounts of him do not contain any reference to great flights of scholarship. Christianity offered a whole way of life and thought to each, but not everyone wanted it all. Again and again in the commentaries, Bede lamented the slowness of his countrymen and their unreadiness to learn Latin. Bede himself became to later generations the ideal of the tirelessly industrious scholar and Alcuin (735–804) held him up as a rare model for the novices of Lindisfarne, who preferred coursing hares to study:

> Look at your treasure of books . . . let the boys be present with praises of the heavenly king and not be digging foxes out of holes or following the fleeting courses of hares. How wicked it is to let slip the services due to Christ and follow the tracks of foxes. He who does not learn when he is young does not teach when he is old. Reflect upon the most noble teacher of your age, the priest Bede, how eager he was to learn when he was young, what praise he has now among men and what greater glory of reward with God.[33]

Bede was a man of exceptional learning but he was not an intellectual elitist. He was concerned that the Gospel should reach all men and he was particularly anxious about the majority of Anglo-Saxons who were nowhere near a monastery school and library. At the end of his life, he urged that basic texts should be translated into English for them. Like Alfred the Great two centuries later, he saw that Christianity was not a matter of magic or of rote; the mind must be filled according to its capacity in order to know the promises and commandments of God and so to know what to follow. And if not everyone would learn Latin, they could learn through translation. In his *Letter to Egbert*, Bede says that he himself had made translations into English for the uneducated to memorize:

> I myself have often given to many ignorant priests both of these, the Creed and the Lord's Prayer, translated into the English language.[34]

In the *Ecclesiastical History*, Bede blamed the first Irish missionary sent from Iona to Northumbria because he could not speak the language of those to whom he was sent, and praised the care taken by Aidan, with the help of King Oswald, that his words should be translated until he could speak English. Everyone had a right to the Gospel and if literacy helped, it should be made available.

It was also important to Bede that everyone should have the chance to speak and he told with special care the story of a dumb boy cured by John of Hexham and given the great and liberating gift of language:

> He told him to put his tongue out and say something; 'Say some word' he said, 'Say *gae*', which in English is the word for assent and agreement. He said at once what the bishop told him to say, the bonds of his tongue being unloosed. The bishop then added the names of the letters: 'Say "A"', and he said it, 'Say "B"', and he said that too. When he had repeated the names of the letters after the bishop, the latter added syllables and words for the youth to repeat after him. When he had repeated them all, one after another, the bishop taught him to say longer sentences, which he did.[35]

Those who could never enter the wide fields of communication through reading and writing, nevertheless could speak, see and hear; they must therefore have access to the Gospel by sight and hearing. Bede described with pleasure two sets of frescoes that adorned the church at Jarrow, brought there by Benedict Biscop from his European travels, because they gave instruction to those who could not read. Bede was concerned with the communication of the Word of God to everyone, and if words helped that was to be praised. The use of reading and writing provided immediate access to the treasures contained in the Bible and the written tradition of the Church. But the Bible was for all and where literacy did not make this immediate access possible, the truth must be made available in other ways.

While his wide sympathies gave him great patience with the poorly equipped, there were however others of intellectual ability who shared his enthusiasm for Latin learning, and turned to him for elucidation of the most abstruse problems. They were not only monks but kings: the letter to Nectan on the calculating of Easter was by Ceolfrith, but by including all of it in the *Ecclesiastical History* Bede suggested that the king of the Picts shared the interests of the Jarrow monks in astronomy. A letter to Wicberht shows

Bede visiting a monastery to explain astronomical matters to the monks at their invitation and later writing to clarify certain points.

Bede's influence went far beyond his own times and his 'scientific' interests caused changes that were fundamental to thought and life in the Middle Ages and beyond but his learning was in no way 'secular'. Each insight was firmly based on the study of the scriptures. Just as he taught grammar from the book of Psalms and justified his work on metrics by referring to Christian poetry and hymns, so all the order he saw in the universe issued from the hand of God and was redeemed in the central moment that changed all time, through the person of Jesus Christ. Piety was a spur in Bede for thought and never the reverse and in this he provides an example of how far the Christian mind can and should be stretched in exploration of the created universe.

Notes

1 HE, V.24, p. 567.

2 Augustine, *On Christian Doctrine*, 2.viii.

3 *Sayings of the Desert Fathers*, trans. Benedicta Ward (Oxford, 1975; 1986), Abba Theodore of Pherme, 1.

4 VSC, viii, p. 180. Cf. my article 'The spirituality of St Cuthbert' in *St Cuthbert, his Cult and his Community to AD 1200*, ed. G. Bonner, D. W. Rollason and C. Stancliffe (London, 1989), pp. 65–77.

5 *Tabernacle*, p. 65.

6 Revelation, preface, col. 133 (Marshall, pp. 8–9).

7 For an admirable discussion of Bede's sources in DO and also the condition of education in eighth-century England see C. W. Jones, DO, Preface, pp. v–xvi.

8 DAM, 1: *De Littera*, pp. 82–5.

9 DST, 12: *De Allegorica*, pp. 161–9.

10 DAM, 23, pp. 138–9.

11 The poem 'On the Day of Judgement' is printed in CCSL CXXII (Turnhout, 1955), pp. 439–44; an Old English version is given in *De Domes Daege*, ed. J. Rawson Lumby (Early English Text Society, London, 1876).

12 *Revelation*, verse preface, col. 134 (Marshall, p. 10).

13 Quoted by Peter Hunter Blair in *Northumbria in the Days of Bede* (London, 1976), p. 156.

14   *The Riddles of Aldhelm*, text and trans. J. Hall Pitman (Yale Studies in English 67; New Haven, Connecticut, 1970), no. 32, pp. 18-19.

15   *A Feast of Creatures: Anglo-Saxon Riddle Songs*, trans. Craig Williamson (London, 1982), no. 24, p. 84.

16   HE, IV.24, pp. 415-21. For a more detailed examination see my article 'Miracles and history' in *Famulus Christi*, pp. 70-7.

17   *Epistola de Obitu Bedae* in HE, pp. 581-7. Cf. E. van K. Dobbie, *Caedmon's Hymn and Bede's Death Song* (New York, 1937); N. Ker, *Medium Aevum* VIII (1939), pp. 40-4.

18   DTR, 1, p. 272.

19   *Chronica Maiora*, AD 1 and AD 33.

20   For a full discussion of the problems involved in the dating of Easter see C. W. Jones, *Bedae Opera de Temporibus* (Cambridge, Massachusetts, 1943), pp. 3-123.

21   HE, III.17, p. 266.

22   *Acts* 1:16, pp. 11-12; quoted by C. Jenkins, 'Bede as exegete and theologian' in BLTW, p. 175.

23   *Revelation* 1:7, col. 150 (Marshall, p. 46).

24   HE(P), p. lix. For an extended note on the significance of numbers in Bede cf. C. Plummer, HE(P) I, pp. lix-lxi.

25   DT, vi (Jones, p. 30), 3; DTR, lxvi (PL 90, 520-1).

26   For an illuminating discussion of this topic see J. A. Burrows, *The Ages of Man* (Oxford, 1988). (See also Chapter 5, pp. 114-16.)

27   *Letter to Plegwine*, p. 315; trans. M. T. Carroll, *The Venerable Bede: his Spiritual Teachings* (Washington, DC, 1946), pp. 44-5.

28   *Revelation*, cols. 197-203.

29   DNR, III.v-ix. For discussion of Bede and his observation of the natural world cf. Wesley M. Stevens, *Bede's Scientific Achievement* (Jarrow, 1985).

30   DNR, IX.

31   HE, I.1, p. 17.

32   HE, IV.3, pp. 339-41.

33   Alcuin, *Letter* 29; trans. Stephen Allott in *Alcuin of York* (York, 1974), p. 40.

34   *Letter to Egbert* (Whitelock), pp. 737-8.

35   HE, V.2, pp. 457-9.

3

Bede and the Bible

The basic teaching of grammar and arithmetic, all the work of the classroom, everything involved in establishing firm structures through which to apprehend reality, were a means to an end for Bede and that end was the study of the Sacred Page. He described it himself as the first duty of his entire life, 'applying myself entirely to the study of the Scriptures', and when he listed his own works, it was his commentaries on the Scriptures which he put first. He himself had been well taught, or at any rate had learned well, and his mind was set towards going further into that 'other country' which Latin and the Bible had opened up for him through study of the commentaries of the Latin Fathers of the Church on the Scriptures. He explored the country before he began to make a map for others to follow. In his description of his own life, after stating his primary work as attention to Scripture he followed it with 'learning' which he put first as his 'delight', and added 'writing, and teaching' second. But the context that he gave for his studies was 'singing in church' and in this structure of the Divine Office he had what must be called the primary source for his scholarship. The Office was composed almost exclusively of words from the Scriptures, while the Office of Matins continually presented him with readings from the Fathers, and though these were supplemented by private reading of fuller texts later, it is significant that Bede's approach to Scripture came first from the daily experience of its use in worship; as well as learning through reading he was learning by singing daily in choir. The commentaries of the Fathers on the Scriptures encountered in this context of prayer were the light of

Bede's own life and thought before he recast them into forms which could become windows through which the 'eastern light' of the early Church could fall upon the Sacred Page newly opened for the 'western darkness' of Anglo-Saxon England.

BEDE'S USE OF THE BIBLE

Bede had the opportunity for profound study of the Bible and he dedicated himself to using it to the full. Through the journeys of Benedict Biscop and Ceolfrith a library had been built up at Wearmouth–Jarrow that made his work possible. They had brought back from the Mediterranean world 'a great mass of books', 'a large supply of sacred books'.[1] The most important of these manuscripts were the copies of the books of the Old and New Testaments in Latin. Very soon, the monks were at work to make more copies: Latin texts of the Bible were vital to the conversion of England, and the work of the monks who were literate was to make copies, whether elaborate gospel-books for use in church, the great pandects such as the *Codex Amiatinus* which Ceolfrith took with him on his last journey[2] or the smaller books for the use of individual readers. Bede's Bible texts can be reconstructed from his commentaries, both through the biblical sections which are quoted in part or in full before they are discussed and from Bede's quotations within his commentaries. He used the Vulgate text of Jerome, with delight at the contact this gave him with the Hebrew text, but referred also to older Latin versions; and in at least one case he was well acquainted with the Greek text of the New Testament.[3]

The biblical texts were not a separate and pious part of Bede's study. For him, the text of the Bible was 'the bread of life' and in his study of the Scriptures for himself he was never static in his approach. As his mind reached out to explore dimensions of space, time and history, at the same time it was concentrated upon the elucidation of the text of the Bible. His work on metrical forms was an introduction to the articulation of the Scriptures in church and his work on grammar was a part of his concern with the words as well as the sounds of the text. All his work for the calculation of time centred on the fact of redemption, while his interest in both grammar and in history led him to explore every word, every name, every place in the texts and to re-evaluate them as other texts came to his hand. This was especially so when he was able to use a Greek text to correct his first comments on the Acts of the Apostles,[4] and it is another mark of his extraordinary genius that he learned enough Greek to do so when Theodore and Hadrian had begun to make such learning a known part of the curriculum only a few years before his birth. Nor was Greek, the language of the New Testament, the only sacred language to attract his attention. Through Jerome he was aware of the importance of the Hebrew text of the Old Testament and while he knew Hebrew only through the works of others, it is again a sign of his acute mind that he grasped its importance and tried to do as well as he could with it. Such linguistic work was not done as an exercise in arid scholarship; it was a part of his penetration through the words of the sacred text to its meaning, and his commentaries are equally full of a devout pondering on the text, which at times formed itself into prayers. For instance, in his commentary on the gospel of Luke, before beginning his comments on Luke 11:14, 'He was casting out a devil and it was dumb', Bede reflected on a previous verse, in which Christ thanked his Father for 'hiding these things from the wise and prudent and revealing them unto babes' (Luke 10:21), and identifying the 'devil that was dumb' with the 'spirit of the proud', he inserted into the text a prayer for himself:

> Since the fourth section of the gospel I am explaining begins with the reading about how the spirit of pride was cast out by the finger of God, I humbly beseech your mercy, O Christ, that your good spirit may lead me in a right path (Psalm 142(143):10) . . . and having cast out evil from me may I keep the commandments of my God (Psalm 118(119):115) and by opening the eyes of my soul (Psalm 118(119):18) may I, a devout reader, begin to behold the wondrous things of thy law.[5]

The priority for Bede was always the practical one of prayer; his commentaries were meditations on the Scriptures leading to conversion of life through prayer. If the extracts from the psalter are his, there is here another instance of the way in which he gave to Scripture its most important place, that of providing a language through which to listen to and speak with God.[6]

BEDE AND THE FATHERS

Bede continually read the Bible and knew most of it, if not all, by heart, so that he had in his mind the complete text which he could use as a concordance; every page of his commentaries shows him at work in this way, constantly placing sentences from different parts of the

Scriptures together, to illuminate one another. But Bede did not read only the Scriptures; his abbots had brought other texts from the south. The commentaries of the Fathers of the Church enabled him to read the Scriptures in the light of the experience of his predecessors and to follow in their footsteps in his own elucidation of the Sacred Page:

> I have written out of the works of the venerable fathers or in conformity with their meaning and interpretation.[7]

He used the works of the early Latin Fathers, for instance, Cyprian, Hilary, Fulgentius, Cassiodorus, Cassian, Isidore, the tracts of Julian of Eclanum and explanations of the book of Revelation by Tyconius and Proserpius, as well as a very large proportion of the writings of Jerome, Augustine, Gregory and Ambrose, whom he was the first to designate as the four Latin Fathers of the Church.[8] Nor was he without some knowledge of the Greek Fathers. For instance, he defended his interpretation of Acts 11:7–8, by reference to a Greek Father:

> I know that I have been blamed by some because I said that this sentence could be understood in two ways. To these I briefly reply that what I wrote about this sentence in my previous volume I did not put forth from my own understanding but took from the words of a master holy and in all things unreprovable, Gregory Nazianzen.[9]

When Bede quoted from the Fathers in some commentaries at least he drew attention to the fact by putting their initials in the margins: 'AV' (Augustine), 'AM' (Ambrose), 'HR' (Jerome), or 'GR' (Gregory) a procedure he explained to Bishop Acca in his letter which accompanied his commentary on Luke: it was done 'lest I be accused of stealing from my predecessors and proposing their views as if they were my own'.[10] In the preface to his commentary on Mark, he urged the reader 'if he should deem these words of mine worth copying' to transcribe also the initial he had placed in the margins, a request rarely followed.

The most usual method of doing theology in the early Church was through commentary on the Scriptures and it was in that tradition that Bede read the text of the Bible. He says he worked first 'for my own benefit' and the pages of his commentaries are full of profoundly personal meditation on the Scriptures, formed both directly from reading the Fathers but even more by the constant immersion of his mind in the daily Office, which reinforced the 'spiritual' understanding of the words which he found so predominant in patristic commentary. The fact that the liturgy of the Christian Church in the West has always been taken almost exclusively from the Old as well as the New Testament, especially from the Psalms, necessitated a profoundly allegorical approach to the texts. The yearly, weekly, daily recitation of the Scriptures within this liturgical framework set the minds of the participants into a spiritual interpretation by which they instinctively discovered Christ and the Church in every phrase of the Bible.

Moreover, from youth Bede had known the allegorical interpretation of the Scriptures not only through words but also through pictures.[11] Twice Benedict Biscop had brought to his monasteries paintings for the walls of the churches and Bede thought them worth describing in some detail:

> He brought back many holy pictures of the saints to adorn the church of St Peter he had built: a painting of the Mother of God, the blessed Mary ever Virgin, and one of each of the twelve apostles which he fixed round the central arch on a wooden entablature reaching from wall to wall; pictures of incidents in the gospels with which he decorated the south wall and scenes from St John's vision of the Apocalypse for the north wall.[12]

Such decoration was traditional in the churches of Rome, Ravenna and Constantinople. It was done so that the walls of the church themselves became a silent, visual 'word of God', giving each worshipper a sense of joining in the life of heaven, as well as offering instruction about the mysteries of faith. The presence of these scenes from the Apocalypse at Jarrow were welcomed by Bede as giving instruction to the illiterate but may also have influenced Bede himself at least subconsciously in that one of his earliest commentaries was on that book. Later, the abbot also set up 'a set of pictures for the monastery and the church of the blessed apostle Paul [i.e. Jarrow]' which was even closer to Bede's patristic learning. They consisted in

> scenes very skilfully arranged to show how the Old Testament foreshadowed the New: in one set for instance, the picture of Isaac carrying the wood on which he was to be burnt as a sacrifice was placed immediately below that of Christ carrying the cross on which he was about to suffer. Similarly the Son of Man lifted up on the Cross was paired with the serpent raised up by Moses in the desert.

This theme of Isaac as a type of Christ was used in the liturgy for Good Friday and for Easter night, and such a juxtaposition of Old and New Testaments was the favourite method of Bede's own commentaries. When he preached a sermon at Epiphany on the miracle at Cana, he referred to the story of the sacrifice of Isaac as a type of the sacrifice of the Cross in precisely the same way as both the frescoes and the liturgy:

> God tested the obedience of Abraham by ordering him to offer as a sacrifice his only son whom he loved ... in the offering of his beloved only son we understand the passion of Him of whom the Father spoke, saying, 'This is my beloved Son in whom I am well pleased' (Matthew 3:17).[13]

BEDE'S METHOD

The basis of Bede's commentaries was that he, like his predecessors, saw all Scripture as the work of one author, God, and a result of this was not only that the New Testament was seen to fulfil the Old, though that was certainly his conviction, but even more it followed from this that any part of either Testament could be used to illuminate any other part. Moreover, the Bible, though a unique book, was for Bede a part of the whole created universe, and all human skills had to be centred upon it. The commentaries on the Scriptures were not therefore isolated from Bede's other works; they were all the creative work of one programme. In each of Bede's commentaries, there are the same elements at work as in his other writings: there is a careful examination of the text before him, for grammar and primary meaning, with reference as far as possible to the Greek text of the Bible and to the Hebrew through Jerome's Latin. There is concern to establish what happened or what was being said; then there is a consideration of the words in the light of the rest of the Scriptures, and then, especially though not exclusively, in the commentaries on the books of the Old Testament, an exploration of the meaning the texts have about the doctrine of Christ and its application to the reader's own life. Figurative expressions are examined for their inner meaning and any number in particular is given meaning beyond itself. Behind all study for Bede lay a delight in the record of Christian revelation, linked indissolubly with both learning and living. This was not a method he invented but that which he found in the way the Fathers had studied the Scriptures. In his treatise *On Christian Doctrine* Augustine of Hippo had proposed as a first step in studying the Scriptures that love of God and neighbour in living out Christian life went together with reading and expounding the Scriptures; then, the diligent student should 'first read all of them'.[14] The next step was to learn as much of them as possible by heart; and then to be aware at least of problems the texts present by being written in other languages:

> Against unknown literal signs the sovereign remedy is a knowledge of languages. And Latin-speaking men ... need two others for a knowledge of the Divine Scriptures, Hebrew and Greek.

Those who had difficulty with this should at least compare different translations into Latin to elucidate obscure phrases. He suggested a thorough examination of

> the nature of animals, or stones or plants or other things which are often used in the Scriptures for the purpose of constructing similitudes,

and recommended a knowledge of the significance of numbers as essential. This programme was that of Bede also. Poetic expressions in the text for Augustine as for Bede were to be explored according to the 'art of grammar' and the 'spiritual' meaning expounded last and only after much careful study.

The Bible was a unique book but it was not a dead letter. The meaning of the text for the writers of it, the historical context, the grammatical meaning, were merely for Bede a beginning of understanding. The Bible was to be read within the tradition of the Church under the continual guidance of the Holy Spirit who would guide

> spiritual teachers and interpreters of both Testaments who, according to the word of the Lord, bring forth from his treasures things new and old.[15]

Bede saw his work as part of a tradition of Bible commentary by which the word of God was continually explored and absorbed in the present and it was to this end that he read and used the Fathers of the Church who had commented on the Sacred Page before him. Bede has been said to lack originality, to have compiled merely a catena of previous authorities in his commentaries, and indeed originality was for him hardly a virtue. He himself insisted that he was repeating what had been said by the Fathers but in this he did himself a disservice. The compilation of texts was for Bede no more than a beginning, a part of his whole exploration of truth. If he found comments of predecessors that were of value, he used and transcribed them as they stood; it may well be that a collection of extracts from the Fathers was always, where possible, his basis for the study of a book of the Bible. Examples survive of his collections of 'authorities', for instance in his seventh book on the Song of Songs, but Bede had no doubt that his own words as well as those of the Fathers could be tools of divine purpose. The comments of the Fathers were judiciously selected, emended and juxtaposed. By this work, Bede provided a working text for those who had no access to the original texts as he did, but he added to them 'some token of my own efforts as the Author of Light revealed them'.[16] At the end of his prefatory letter to his commentary on the book of Revelation he describes his use of authorities:

> Now we have followed on our part the sense of this author [Tyconius] but in so doing we have omitted some things which he inserted beyond the purpose in order to be more compendious, and we have taken care to add many more which to him ... appeared plain and unworthy of investigation; and this we have done so far as we have been able, either by the tradition of the masters, or the recollection of reading, or even our own capacity; for this, too, is among the commandments which we have received, to return to the Lord with usury the talents which have been committed to us.[17]

In some cases, Bede had previous commentaries upon which to draw; in others, he knew of no predecessor. It is significant of the genuine and original contribution of Bede to theology that so large a part of the twelfth-century collection of standard comments of the Fathers on the Bible, the *Glossa Ordinaria*, should have been taken from his works.

THE SPIRITUAL SENSE OF THE SCRIPTURES

In his daily exposure to the Office and in his reading of the Fathers, Bede absorbed the understanding of the Bible as a doorway into another world of the spirit. The spiritual sense of the Scriptures was as important to Bede as the literal grammatical meaning and he came to regard it as vital. In the prefatory letter to Acca before his commentary on Samuel, Bede says that he had been thinking about his own reasons for making such a commentary, and gives a clear account of his method:

The whole series of the divine scriptures is interpreted in a fourfold way. In all holy books one should ascertain what everlasting truths are there intimated, what deeds are narrated, what future events are foretold and what commands or counsels are there contained. . . . The word of the heavenly oracle can be received in either an historical, or allegorical, a tropological (that is, moral) or even an anagogical sense.

It is history when is recorded in clear words according as it was literally said or done, e.g. the people of Israel saved from Egypt is reported to have made a tabernacle of the Lord in the wilderness.

It is allegory when the presence of Christ or the sacraments of the church are designated by mystical words or events, e.g. when Isaias says 'and there shall come forth a rod out of the stem of Jesse and a flower shall rise up out of his root' (Isaiah 11:1), he means the Virgin Mary shall be born of the root of David and Christ shall be born out of her stock. This may be illustrated also with regard to events, e.g. the people saved from slavery in Egypt through the blood of the Lamb signifies the church freed by the passion of Christ from the domination of the devil.

It is tropology, that is, a moral manner of speaking, when appearing in either literal or figurative language, it appertains to moral instruction and correction, e.g. literal, as when John gives the warning, 'my little children, let us not love in word nor in tongue but in deed and in truth'; in figures as when Solomon says 'at all times let your garments be white and let not oil depart from your head' (Ecclesiastes 9:8), which is to be interpreted, at all times let your work be clean and let not charity depart from your heart.

It is anagogy, that is, a form of speech looking to higher things, which discusses, either in plain or in mystical words, future rewards and in what the future life of heaven consists e.g. in plain words, 'Blessed are the pure of heart for they shall see God' (Matthew 5:8) but in mystical words, 'Blessed are they that wash their robes, that they may have the right to the tree of life and may enter in at the gates of the city' (Revelation 22:14), which means, blessed are they who cleanse their thoughts and actions so that they may have the power to see the Lord Christ who says, 'I am the way the truth and the life' and they who through the teaching and example of the preceding fathers enter into the kingdom of heaven.[18]

Bede was describing here a fourfold understanding of Scripture, but earlier he explored a more complex system. In his prefatory letter to Hwaetberht on the Book of Revelation, he had suggested that his commentary could be done according to the seven rules of Tyconius, which he had found in Augustine's *On Christian Doctrine*. After an analysis of the book into sections and themes, he concluded,

> I have also thought that the seven rules of Tyconius, a man of the most learning among those of his sect, should be briefly enumerated inasmuch as those who are eager to learn receive much help from them in understanding the Scriptures.[19]

In depending on someone he knew to be connected with the heresy of Donatism Bede ran a risk which later he would be reluctant to do, when he had experienced the condemnation of his own views as heretical by those he never ceased to regard as ignorant and stupid. His early freedom and assurance here led him to criticize not only Tyconius but even Augustine when, perhaps mischievously, he quotes the rules and applies the second rule directly to the seven angels (Revelation 1:20), the very instance Augustine gave to show that not every point could be elucidated by Tyconius and his method.

The allegorical, mystical interpretation of the Scriptures meant much to Bede, but it was based on an equal concern for the grammatical meaning of the text. Moreover, he followed even more carefully another piece of advice which he found in Augustine's *On Christian Doctrine*: the primacy of charity in the understanding of a text. It is this which coloured all his writing; the use of rules or patterns lay always below the surface, as a tool rather than ostentatious display, to be used as appropriate for this other and more vital end:

> The church takes from the Lord the divine gift of faith and love ... until all the earth is set on fire with love of the kingdom of heaven.[20]

BEDE ON THE NEW TESTAMENT

It seems probable that Bede compiled texts from his reading of the Fathers for his own use before he either taught or wrote, but for many of his commentaries on the New Testament he had no predecessor. His earliest works were commentaries on the book of Revelation and the seven catholic epistles, the most mystical and the most prosaic books of the New Testament and while he had authorities to consult for the former, for the latter this was not the case except on one instance. Later, he commented on Acts twice, since after some years he wrote a second commentary as a correction of his first. He wrote also an elucidation of the place-names of Palestine. Beyond that, 'with great fear and trembling', he commented on two gospels, Luke and Mark, where he already had great predecessors, notably Ambrose and Gregory. In all his writings, Bede again and again used the letters of Paul who was to him 'the apostle', and who was moreover the patron of his monastery at Jarrow. Bede called Paul *famulus Dei* (servant of God) as he called himself *famulus Christi*, but it seems that no new commentary of Bede on St Paul survives and perhaps he never made one: in the list of his works he says 'On the apostle [Paul] I have transcribed in order whatever I found in the works of St Augustine'.[21]

Commentary on Revelation

Bede's earliest commentary was on the book of the Revelation of St John the Divine. Like the *De Temporum Ratione* it was dedicated to Hwaetberht, the 'Eusebius' of Jarrow. In the list of his works at the end of the *Ecclesiastical History* written after 731 Bede listed among his commentaries, 'On the Apocalypse of St John: three books', but it is possible to date its composition more precisely than that. In the prefatory letter, Bede did not address Hwaetberht as abbot, which he became in 716; moreover, in a letter Bede wrote to Acca, who had become bishop of Hexham in 710, he addressed him as bishop and referred again to Hwaetberht as 'brother':

> The exposition of the Apocalypse of the holy Evangelist John which, written at the request of our brother Eusebius and contained in three books, I intend to copy and send you soon.[22]

Thus it seems that the Revelation commentary was completed between 710 and 716, when Bede was already ordained priest and between thirty-seven and forty-three years of age. It was a short and very popular work, of which about 73 manuscripts survive. It

51

provided a clear guide to a very difficult but attractive text. With it Bede sent a prefatory letter to Hwaetberht and a poem *Exul ab humano* ('An exile from the busy haunts of men'), deprecating his own attempts at elucidation and praising John the Apostle. It is here, in the preface to what was perhaps his first theological work, that Bede listed the rules of Tyconius and at certain points in the commentary he refers to the interpretation of the Book of Revelation by Tyconius, as one among other possibilities; at no point does he attempt to apply the 'rules of Tyconius' systematically to the whole text, and indeed he drew upon commentaries other than that of Tyconius.

Bede attributed the book of Revelation to the apostle John, as he did both the gospel of St John and the epistles of St John on which he commented soon after, seeing in them all the work of one especially close to the Lord, who, even more than the other apostles, knew the humanity of the Saviour:

> The apostles could not doubt that this was a true body, inasmuch as they proved its genuineness not only by seeing but also by touching it, particularly John himself who being accustomed to recline on his lap at supper touched his members more freely as he was nearer.[23]

Bede did not interpret the book of Revelation as prophesying the end of the world in the fashion of later commentators, but saw it as an allegory on the present troubles and future rewards of the Church, as he says at the beginning of his letter to Hwaetberht, describing the text as

> The Apocalypse of St John, in which God was pleased to reveal by words and figures the wars and internal tumults of the church.

He then expanded this comment:

> The Revelation of St John seems to me . . . to be divided into several sections. In the first of these . . . he sees one like unto the son of man clothed with the church, who after he has related what has happened or is about to happen, to the seven churches in Asia in particular, recounts the general conflicts and victories of the whole church.[24]

The commentary contains much that Bede copied directly from his predecessors, but there is also much that is his own. Here his fascination with numbers had full play. The number seven, the perfect number, seemed to him to give the shape of each part of the text which he saw as falling into seven main parts: the seven seals, the seven angels with trumpets and the seven plagues, while the sixth section has the 'condemnation of the great whore, that is, of the ungodly city' and the seventh saw 'the ornament of the Lamb's wife, the holy Jerusalem, coming down out of heaven from God'. This led Bede to comment:

> So in mystic wisdom he [John] almost always retains this number, for neither in his gospel nor in his epistle is the same John accustomed to say anything with remissness or brevity.[25]

In this first work Bede was no strict adherent of even the most popular of precedents and he was challenged on the orthodoxy of his interpretation here of the symbols of the evangelists: in commenting on Revelation 4:7 he wrote:

> Matthew is intended as the lion, in that he describes the ancestral line of regal dignity in Christ, who also has conquered as the lion of Judah, for 'Judah is the lion's whelp'; ... Luke is intended as the calf, which was the great victim under the Law ... the face of a man signifies Mark, who only relates simply the actions of the man Christ, and the eagle is John.[26]

These 'four living creatures', the lion, the calf, the eagle and the face of a man, which he found described in Revelation had been based by the author on the description in Ezekiel of the four 'living creatures':

> Each had the face of a man in front, the four had the face of a lion on the right side, the four had the face of an ox on the left side, and the four had the face of an eagle at the back (Ezekiel 1:10).

In Revelation they became:

> Four beasts full of eyes before and behind. The first beast was like a lion, the second beast like a calf, the third beast had the face of a man, and the fourth beast was like a flying eagle (Revelation 4:6–7).

These creatures were well-known in the early Church as symbols of the four evangelists but the interpretation of them was not usually that proposed by Bede. In Northumbria before Bede's day the order best known was that given by Jerome in which Matthew was the man; Mark the lion; Luke the calf and John the eagle, an order used in the illuminations of both the Lindisfarne Gospels and the Book of Kells. But in this commentary and elsewhere Bede followed Augustine in making Mark the man and Matthew the lion and Luke the calf, since he agreed with Augustine's opinions about the leading characteristics of each evangelist. The lion symbolized Matthew's gospel because it contains the genealogy of Christ in the royal line of the House of Judah; Luke's gospel was represented by the sacrificial calf because of the priestly element introduced at the beginning by the priest Zacharias in the Temple; and Mark's gospel was symbolized by the face of a man because of not being either of the other two, but describing Christ directly; there was no conflict about the use of the eagle as the emblem of John. In this view, which he reaffirmed and expanded in his commentary on Luke, Bede was accused of being an innovator, and he replied elsewhere rather sharply that more careful reading would have shown his detractors that it was not 'my own new explanation but an old explanation from a venerated church father [Augustine]'.[27]

Even in this early work, Bede was not fanciful at the expense of teaching; he used allegory only as a servant of his main purpose of edification. Here was his first public exercise in biblical commentary, but although it concerned the book most full of mysterious symbols, his interpretation was made according to his understanding of the whole of the Scriptures as an interrelated message from God to man. Each section was understood in relation to other parts of the Bible and he refers to the Cross as the key to understanding the text when he wrote:

> The Lord by his passion proved that the Covenant of both Testaments was fulfilled in himself.[28]

This living presence of Christ to the reader or hearer was guaranteed and in one sentence Bede summed up his understanding of the inerrability of the Scriptures:

> Whether you attend to the letter or seek for an allegory, in the Gospel you will always find light.[29]

In commenting on the harps of Revelation 14:2, Bede examined their significance in a way entirely typical of this approach: he used another part of the New Testament, Galatians 5:4, and combined it with one of the best-known of patristic interpretations by which the harp was seen as the human body, as Augustine put it, on the psaltery gut is stretched ... the flesh is crucified ... let him stretch himself out on the wood and be dried from the lust of the flesh ... The more the strings are stretched the more sharply they sound ... he stretched himself, Christ touched him and the sweetness of truth sounded.[30]

Bede turned this allegory into a very similar and direct phrase:

all the saints are God's harpers for 'by crucifying the flesh with its lusts' (Galatians 5:4) they praise him in the psaltery and the harp.

Earlier he used the same image:

by 'harps' in which strings are stretched on wood are represented bodies prepared to die and by 'bowls', hearts expanded in breadth of love.[31]

This exploration of inner truth with an immediate and personal application to life also shaped his comment on Revelation 9:23:

Our works and words no doubt may be known to men but with what intention they are accomplished and to what end we desire to come by their means, He alone knows who sees what each one thinks and in what he takes delight.[32]

There are two entirely personal comments in this treatise: after his long explanation of the jewels of the city he apologizes for its length with a disarming sentence, which shows the scholar immersed in his work, aware that what he had just written was out of proportion but also aware of how much there is to do beyond this:

This explanation of the precious stones I seem, perhaps, to have set out more fully than the method of explanation by clauses requires. For it was not necessary to explain carefully their composition and where they came from, and then to inquire into their sacramental meaning and furthermore to treat of their order and number. But as regards the profoundness of the subject itself I seem to myself to have said very few things and that briefly and summarily.

This sense of having fallen by accident into writing a book within a book was followed by one of the personal requests for prayers which recur in all his works:

I beg the reader, if he sees that I have trod in the right path, to give thanks to God; and if he discovers that it is otherwise than I desired, let him pray the Lord to pardon my error.[33]

Secondly, he inserted a prayer of his own when commenting on those that 'die in the Lord' (Revelation 14:13) in an equally personal manner:

> I thank you, Lord Jesus, that you have made blessed in heaven those who die for you on earth and how much more those who lay down their blissful lives both in and for your faith.[34]

Commentary on the Catholic Epistles

After his explanations of the most mysterious book of the New Testament, Bede's next work was a series of commentaries on some of its most prosaic works, the catholic epistles. In this he was again concerned with the preachers and teachers who had to expound the texts to others. Bede knew of no other commentaries by any of the Fathers on these texts except on 1 John where he had a predecessor in Augustine. It was this commentary, based on that of Augustine, which he finished first and sent to Acca with his commentary on Acts soon after 709. In the *Ecclesiastical History* he lists these commentaries after his work on Acts: 'on the seven catholic epistles: one book each', but this list is not chronological. Bede wrote these commentaries as a group; they were often copied, and usually together.

Bede drew from the texts very clear instructions about behaviour, and used the spiritual understanding of the text to expand the plain sense for the use of the reader. For instance, in commenting on 'you yourselves as living stones are builded up into a spiritual house' (1 Peter 2:5) he described the Church present, future and past:

> Just as rows of stones in a wall are held up by others so all the faithful in the church are held up by the righteousness of those who went before them, they themselves by their teaching and help hold up those who come after even to the last righteous man.[35]

This sense of the timelessness of the Church caused him to see the letters as directly sent from the apostles to the reader, without any further concern for their historical context:

> We also if we can truly say to God that in your sight we are dwellers on earth and travellers like our fathers (Ps 38(39):12) ought to believe that the letters of blessed Peter were written to us as well as to them and to read them as having been sent to us.[36]

This sense of continuity had a special application to Bede's clerical readers:

Just as the Lord ordered blessed Peter to care for his entire flock, that is, the church, so Peter himself justifiably commands the succeeding pastors of the church to protect with careful government the flock that each has with him.[37]

It was Bede's care for the teachers among his readers that caused him to include in each commentary on the epistles warnings against, and explanations of the errors of, the best-known of the heretics of the early Church, whether Jovinian, Pelagius, Arius, Photius, Mani or Ebion:

They rightly bring upon themselves swift destruction who denying their Redeemer refuse to glorify him by confessing him truly and to carry him in their body by doing what is right, a thing that all heretics do.[38]

Soon after he wrote this, Bede was to meet criticism levelled at him for heresy himself; it must have seemed especially hard in view of his condemnation here of every kind of heresy known to him.

There is one section only in these commentaries in which Bede writes in the first person and it has a curious ring to it:

Prayers are hindered by the conjugal duty because as often as I perform what is due to my wife I am not able to pray. But if according to another statement of the apostle we must 'pray without ceasing' (1 Thessalonians 5:17) I must therefore never gratify my conjugal duty lest I be hindered at my hour of prayer in which I am ordered always to persevere.[39]

Such a passage comes strangely in the first person from such a monk, but there is a similar section in his commentary on Luke and the hundredfold reward for those who leave all to follow Christ where he again resorts to the first person:

Formerly I possessed a wife in the lustful passion of desire and now I possess her in honourable sancification and true love of Christ.[40]

Perhaps his own assurance of celibacy gave him a certain freedom to make use of this rhetorical device. The fact that he adds 'A woman is one but chastity gives a hundred fold in merit' might suggest a certain contempt for the flesh; but Bede was no dualist, and in his commentary on Genesis he expressed approval for the institution of marriage:

> If, however, the human race increases and is multiplied with the blessing of God, how greatly do they deserve to be cursed who prohibit marriage and condemn the following of a divine ordinance as if it had been discovered by the devil.[41]

It was all a question of vocation within the Church, where the married, the widowed and the celibate all receive blessings according to their state. If Bede praised virginity most of all, it was his own vocation and it was an opinion he certainly shared with the Fathers:

> But more to be honoured and worthy of greater blessing is that virginity which, after the earth has been filled with men, desires with pure mind and body to follow the Lamb whithersoever he shall have gone, that is the Lord Jesus in heaven.[42]

Commentary and Retractation on the Acts of the Apostles

Working in reverse order through the New Testament, Bede included his *Commentary on Acts* in the list of his works: 'On the Acts of the Apostles: two books'. The first book was completed in haste soon after 709 and sent to Bishop Acca with the treatise on the first letter of John, together with a plea from Bede that to comment on the gospel as Acca had suggested was beyond his scope. In his first commentary on Acts Bede used the method now familiar to him: it was done verse by verse, though not all verses were commented on. As in the commentary on Revelation, he considered the proper names of places and people, giving brief explanations, with some extended comment about the inner meaning he found in the text. For instance, he expanded the text of Acts 1:3 into a commentary on the central mystery of salvation, using images found also in the vigil celebrated on Easter night:

> For we are buried with Christ by baptism in death, as if passing through the Red Sea on dry land; it was necessary for us to be led into the wilderness by the Lord who leads us to the kingdom of heaven and rewards us in this present life with his image on the coin of the Holy Spirit as if he had already made us blessed with the rest of jubilee.[43]

All parts of the Scriptures could be called upon to elucidate the text for the immediate use of the reader not only in the concordance of texts from Mark and Luke which he used to fill out the description of the Ascension in Acts, but with many other passages, where quotations from the Old and New Testaments abound.

Twenty years later, Bede sent Acca another tract on Acts: this was his *Retractation on the Books of Acts*. His increasing mastery of Greek and access to Greek manuscripts had shown him errors in his first treatise; he therefore made a second and revised edition. It is a remarkable piece of scholarship, in which Bede can be seen at work on textual matters and commenting in a sophisticated manner on the problems involved:

> I have not yet been able to determine whether some changes and omissions are due to the negligence of the translator or to his use of different words or whether we are dealing with a case of scribes altering the text and omitting words. I hesitate to suppose that the Greek exemplar itself was a faulty one. Let my reader therefore accept whatever comments I make on these matters as scholarly comments and let him not on that account start to correct his own copy of Acts, unless perhaps he discovers a very old manuscript of the Latin version which confirms these comments.[44]

In this commentary, Bede shows his ability as a corrector of texts and also that quality of a great scholar which enabled him to say he was wrong. His grammatical instinct was sound and accounts for most of the alterations, for example:

> I wrote in the previous book that Stephen means 'crowned', nor is what I wrote far from what is true. But, learning more accurately, I have found that Stephen signifies in Greek not 'crowned' but 'a crown', for this name *corona* is, among the Greeks, of a masculine gender and therefore appropriate to a man; but the one who is crowned is called *stephanephoros* i.e. bearing a crown. . . . 'Crown' among the Greeks is also called *stemma*. I have thought this worthy of commemoration because we often find this name Stephen occurring in Latin books, too.[45]

He made, perhaps at the same time, as an appendix a list of the names of the holy places, which he also included in an abbreviated form in the *Ecclesiastical History*, where he says he based it on a book by the Irish monk Adamnan which was circulating in Northumbria in his days. Adamnan had written down his account of the holy places from information given him by a much-travelled Gaulish bishop, Arculf, who had met Adamnan by the chance of shipwreck in Ireland or Iona. Adamnan had given his written account to King Aldfrith, who had had many copies made which would be useful to many and especially to those who live very far from the places where the apostles and patriarchs dwelt and only know about them what they have learned from books.[46]

To this Bede added extracts from Eucherius of Lyons and Josephus's *History of the Jews*. His excuse for including an abbreviated form of this work in his *Ecclesiastical History* is that he was writing about the visit of Adamnan to King Aldfrith, but in fact by inserting it there Bede made sure that it would reach a wider audience than the original treatise added to Acts. It is significant that Bede considered this, alone of his works, suitable for inclusion in both his biblical and his historical works. It is an entirely practical piece of writing, concerned with the names and locations of places mentioned in the Bible, and demonstrated Bede's concern with the historicity of biblical places and people. It further underlines also the sense he had of the continuity between the past and present that in a book concerned with contemporary holy places, he included also this physical account of ancient Palestine.

Commentaries on the Gospels

Bede's other commentaries on the New Testament were on the gospels, on Luke and then on Mark, repeating much of the same material in the second work. It seems that Acca overcame Bede's reluctance to comment on the gospels and, as he says, he produced: 'On the Gospel of Mark: four books; On the Gospel of Luke: six books'. The next work he lists, 'Homilies on the Gospels: two books', should surely be considered with them, both because they were among the most popular of Bede's writings and also for the commentary they provide on parts of the gospels.

As the other part of Luke's work, of which Acts was the first part, the gospel according to Luke was an appropriate work for Bede to undertake after his explanation of Acts. He may already have begun work on Luke when he sent his first commentary on Acts to Acca *c*. 709, at a time when he was also at work on his commentary on Samuel (716). Reluctant as he was to comment on so sacred a text as a gospel, where he had moreover illustrious predecessors, Bede's commentaries show all his accustomed authority and insight. He knew and admired the commentary of Ambrose of Milan, and also used passages from Augustine, Jerome, Hilary and Gregory in his own work. Such quotation was not in any way plagiarism but a sense that if something had previously been written which was of great value, it should be made available. In order to quiet criticisms that he used other men's work without acknowledgement, he gave indications of the sources of his quotations in the margins of these texts, which were sometimes included by copyists and sometimes not. He chose with care from his predecessors with an eye to making them useful to a new audience. He added also much of his own. In the prefatory letter to Acca he struck a solemn note: the reward of this study would be a true vision of God here and hereafter: all that was needed was dedication and hard work:

> For if Moses and all the prophets spake of Christ and how he entered through his bitter passion into his glory, what reason have they to glory in being Christians who according to the measure of their strength neither desire to investigate how the scriptures relate to Christ nor to attain through bearing tribulation to that glory which they want to have with Christ?[47]

The method of Bede's commentary on both Luke and Mark is familiar: he takes the texts verse by verse, first looking at the words of the text and expounding any grammatical difficulty, then applying the meaning to the reader in one or more ways. As always, other parts of the Scriptures are brought in to elucidate the text of Luke; for instance, in expounding Luke 10:23, 'Blessed are the eyes which see the things that you see', Bede refers to Abraham of whom it was said in John 8:56 that he 'rejoiced to see Christ's day'. He then quotes from Isaiah 6:1; Micah 1:1; and Paul, 1 Corinthians 13:12, as well as comparing the same text in Matthew 13:17 with Luke. The eyes that are 'blessed' he concludes are not only those of prophets and apostles in the past but those in the present who

> do not succumb by consenting to the stirrings of their temptations but know how to subdue them by overruling them.[48]

In the two letters Bede wrote to Bishop Acca about his work on Luke he asserted firmly that he meant to break with tradition about the symbols of the evangelists, as he had already done in his commentary on Revelation, and explained in detail why he had chosen to interpret them according to Augustine and not the far better-known Jerome. It had become a matter of personal conviction about the meaning of Luke and the last words of Bede's commentary, like his comments in the preface, were about this sacerdotal theme in Luke. Commenting on the verse 'they were daily in the temple blessing and praising God', he says that since

Luke's gospel was symbolized by the calf of sacrifice, it was right to begin with expounding the sacrifice of Zacharias in the temple, but that it is even more appropriate to end with the sacrifice of praise being offered by the Church:

> The new priesthood of the future ends not in bloody victims but in the praise and blessing of God.[49]

Bede's commentary on the gospel of Mark, which he described in his list of his works as 'on the Gospel of Mark: three books', was made after the commentaries on both Samuel and Luke. He used his previous work on Luke word for word for nearly a third of the text. It must therefore have been written after 716 and was, like so many of his works, addressed to and done for 'the beloved bishop Acca', again with marginal notes wherever he quoted other works.

Different points are stressed in each commentary: for instance, in his comments on Luke's version of the healing of the demoniac boy after the Transfiguration (Luke 9:47–50) Bede referred to similar cures in Matthew and Mark, quoted a comment on the text by Jerome, and compared this liberation from a demon to the forgiveness of sins for all Christians. In commenting on the same incident in Mark, he repeated some of his observations but expanded the more extensive version in Mark, and gave a comment relevant to his readers on the phrase, 'this kind goeth not out but by prayer and fasting' (Mark 9:29):

> Now fasting is a general word, it signifies abstaining not only from food but from all allurements of the flesh and self-restraint from every kind of vicious passion. Likewise, prayer in general consists not only in the words with which we invoke the mercy of God but in everything we do in devout faith to serve our Creator.[50]

THE HOMILIES

In the list of his works, Bede included 'Homilies on the Gospels: two books', which suggests that in his lifetime his sermons were already written in the collection in which they circulated so widely. This does not mean that they were never actually delivered. At times, perhaps in place of one of his abbots during their frequent journeys abroad, Bede would preach to the brothers at Jarrow, either the evening before a festival or during the Mass. Such sermons were written down, presumably by Bede himself either before or after preaching, and perhaps corrected for a wider audience. Some of these he selected for circulation in writing. Presumably he preached on other texts at other times of the year, but these were the sermons he collected together and revised. Each has for its text a verse from one of the gospels and Bede listed them immediately after his gospel commentaries.

The homilies were related to the major turning points in the Church's year, Easter and Christmas. Fifteen were grouped around the feast of the Nativity, with four for Advent, five for Christmas and its octave (i.e. one for the vigil, one each for the three Masses of Christmas Day and one for the octave day), one for Epiphany and five for the Sundays after it. Twenty-one of the sermons related to Easter: seven sermons in Lent; one each for Palm Sunday, Holy Week and Maundy Thursday; two for Holy Saturday; one for the Sunday of Easter; five during Eastertide; one for Ascension; one for Pentecost; and one for the octave of Pentecost. The rest of the sermons are for the feasts of the saints. There are sermons for the feasts of John the Evangelist and the Holy Innocents, which occurred in the week after Christmas, and for the Presentation of Christ in the Temple, which formed part of the Nativity cycle; two sermons were given for feasts of Peter the Apostle, and the apostles Peter and Paul; two were for the feasts of the Birth and the Beheading of John the Baptist, and one for the Roman martyrs John and Paul. Three sermons were for two feasts of local interest at Jarrow, one for the anniversary of the death of Benedict Biscop and two for the anniversary of the dedication of the Church of St Paul at Jarrow. There is also one sermon for Ember Days, which fell within the Easter cycle.

It is no surprise that the largest group of homilies centred on Easter, that central feast to which Bede paid so much attention elsewhere. The sermons for the feast of Christmas also are in line with his work on the calendar. The saints' days were those of major figures in Christian history, with two exceptions: the sermon commemorating the recent founder of Jarrow and Wearmouth, Benedict Biscop, and the sermon for two early martyrs, John and Paul, who may have been especially commemorated both because their names were included in the Canon of the Mass and because of a special devotion to them by Saxon pilgrims who had visited their supposed burial place in Rome in the church built on the Caelian hill. The sermon for Ember Days may have been included by Bede in his collection simply because it is a particularly fine piece of writing about prayer.

Bede's sermons are in the same style as his commentaries; indeed, it is hardly possible to distinguish between homily and commentary. For instance, prayer and fasting, which, as has been seen, Bede urged in his commentary on the gospel of Mark, was a theme which he repeated and expanded in a homily for the Ember Days:

> We cannot otherwise fulfil the command of the apostle to 'pray without ceasing' unless by the gift of God we so direct all our actions, words, thoughts and even our silences so that each may be tempered by regard for him and all may become profitable for our salvation.[51]

This similarity between commentary and homily is not accidental. In all his works, Bede had the same aim in mind; what differed was not the method but the audience. In commenting on Luke 11:9–13, 'Ask and it shall be given you, seek and you shall find', and in his sermon for the Ember Days on the same text, Bede produced a guide to intercession in both. In the commentary, he gave quotations from Augustine and Jerome about prayer and in the homily, though he twice briefly cited Gregory the Great on the same passage, the comments on right and wrong prayer were his own. In both cases, he examined the text and then drew out of it an inner meaning applicable to the readers or hearers. In the commentary, he offered a variety of insights for the use of preachers when constructing their own sermons, but in the homily he was himself the preacher. There, he explained a point about intercession with care and insight into the questions of his contemporaries, with his familiar stress on peace:

> Citizens of the heavenly fatherland who are pilgrims on earth are not forbidden to pray to the Lord for times of peace, for bodily health, for abundance of crops and for the necessities of life, that is, if these things are not sought to excess, and if they are only sought so that with abounding life at present we may reach out more freely to the gifts that are to come. There are some, however, who demand temporal peace and prosperity from their Creator, not in order to obey that Creator with greater dedication of spirit but in order to have more opportunity for feasting and drunkenness and so that they may more easily and freely become slaves to the attraction of fleshly desires. Of such men it is rightly said that they pray in an evil fashion. Truly none who pray in this way deserve to receive what they seek in this evil manner. And so, my beloved

brethren, let us strive both to pray well and to become worthy to receive that for which we pray.[52]

Bede's homily for Easter night is a particularly fine example of his homiletic style. In his commentaries on Luke and Mark and their accounts of the Resurrection, he dealt with each phrase in turn, referring to other parts of the Bible to illuminate the texts, exploring the spiritual as well as the literal meaning, with liberal quotation from the Fathers, and carefully explaining any heretical notions which the text contradicts. In the homily, he collected together all the instances of descriptions of the resurrection appearances of Jesus from all the gospel accounts, illuminated the text by reference to other parts of the scriptures, indicated pitfalls such as 'the heresy of the Corinthians', and then applied the texts directly to the present meeting of the brothers for the celebration of the feast of the Resurrection:

> We must trust in his goodness that this also happens to us, who are far lower than the apostles, so that as often as we are gathered in his name, He is in the midst of us. For his name is Jesus that is our Saviour and when we come together to speak of obtaining our salvation, then we are gathered together in his name.[53]

The theme of the sermon is that which is especially familiar in Bede's work: peace:

> When the Saviour appears in the midst of his disciples, he immediately bestows on them the joys of peace, repeating now in the fulfilled glory of his immortality that which he had committed to them as the special pledge of their salvation when he was himself about to undergo his passion saying unto them, 'Peace I leave with you, my peace I give unto you' ... for the whole mission of our Redeemer in the flesh was to restore peace to the world.[54]

The special mark of the homilies is the direct application of biblical passages to a specific audience; whereas the commentaries gave other preachers the material for sermons, here Bede himself made the application.

THE OLD TESTAMENT

However practical and useful Bede's commentaries on the New Testament were, it was in his commentaries on the books of the Old Testament that his theology expanded and flourished. To present the spiritual meaning of these books was overwhelmingly important if the Anglo-Saxons were to be edified by them and not just filled with admiration for warlike kings protected by God, a concept which tied in far too well with their unregenerate selves.[55] Even more than with the New Testament, not all the books of the Old Testament had been expounded by the Fathers and even fewer of them were either available or comprehensible to Anglo-Saxon Christians. But even more, Bede himself found here the place for his most profound understanding of Christianity. Suddenly absorbed by the text of Samuel, he was ready to cobble together a commentary on Acts and postpone work on Luke, exploring with a new freedom the spiritual, mystical meaning of the Old Testament Sacred Page.

Of the commentaries on the Old Testament which he listed at the end of the *Ecclesiastical History*, most have survived:

> The beginning of Genesis up to the birth of Isaac and the casting out of Ishmael: four books. The tabernacle, its vessels and the priestly vestments: three books. The first book of Samuel to the death of Saul: four books. On the building of the temple, an allegorical interpretation like the others: two books. On the book of Kings: thirty questions. On the Proverbs of Solomon: three books. On the Song of Songs: seven books . . . On Ezra and Nehemiah: three books. On the Song of Habbakuk: one book. On the book of the blessed father Tobias, an allegorical explanation concerning Christ and the Church: one book.

What are so far lost may have been collections of notes rather than full commentaries:

> On Isaiah, Daniel, the twelve prophets and part of Jeremiah: chapter divisions taken from the treatise of Jerome. . . . Also summaries on the lessons on the Pentateuch of Moses, on Joshua and Judges, on the book of Kings and Chronicles, on the book of the blessed father Job, on Proverbs, Ecclesiastes and the Song of Songs, on the prophets Isaiah, Ezra and Nehemiah.

The books of the Old Testament provided Bede with a challenge and a free field for exploration of the spiritual sense of the texts. It was work exactly suited to his mind and he produced mystical commentary of a high order from almost every page. The task of drawing out meaning relevant to the reader and at the same time expressive of the mystery of Christ seemed to him a great responsibility and one in which he immersed himself gladly. The central fact of the passion of Christ provided for him a key to all the Scriptures; he exclaimed, 'By the Lord's passion the abyss of the Scriptures is made open to us'.[56] It is in these commentaries that the most profound of Bede's doctrinal and devotional thought is to be found.

Commentary on Samuel

Bede's earliest commentary on the Old Testament was on Samuel. He completed three books before the departure of Ceolfrith for Rome in 716 and the fourth book soon after. The commentary extends from the first verse of Samuel with the calling of the child Samuel to the account of the death and burial of Saul and Jonathan. He used Jerome for the meaning of the Hebrew names in the text and added an alphabetical list of the meanings of these culled from Jerome almost entirely, but while he quoted constantly from other parts of Scripture to illuminate passages he referred only to Jerome and Gregory the Great in his commentary, and that sparingly.

Perhaps the work appealed to Bede by instinct, since its author has been described as 'the father of history'. He made it clear in his preface to Bishop Acca that he was not concerned with the literal sense of the work but with 'true history', that is, interpretation according to Christ. In a note near the beginning of his commentary he warned the 'careful reader' that there is not only one interpretation of each part of the text: 'true history' has many faces and need not be consistent. For instance, he wrote,

> the childish simplicity of Samuel and the blind torpor of Eli signify the humility of the Lord and Saviour and the stupid perfidy of the Jews,

but the words of the child Samuel in the same passage, 'Here am I, for you called me', should be

> truly and certainly read as predicting the Incarnation of Christ.[57]

In the preceding paragraph, moreover, he had already connected the phrase 'here am I' with the Johannine sense of the abiding of Christ with the Father, 'I and the Father are one'. This use of Christological interpretations supported by texts from other parts of the Scriptures is sustained through the whole book, a unique *tour de force*. Indeed, at least twice Bede himself inserted a comment about the difficulty of the work. But it was a work much needed if the Anglo-Saxon preachers were to make full use of the text. As Bede remarked to Acca in his letter, the apostle Paul had said that 'whatsoever things were written aforetime were written for our learning' (Romans 15:4) but the historical fact that Helcana had two wives was scarcely of ultimate concern to monks who did not even have one. An interior meaning had to be sought in such words, and in this case, he saw the two wives as symbols of the Synagogue and the Church, both betrothed to Christ.[58]

Not all the commentary was newly wrought in Bede's fertile brain. In this section of the Bible there were passages which already had well-known Christological interpretations, for instance, the fight of David against Goliath was presented in art, hymns, and the liturgy as an image of the fight of Christ against the devil, and this is the meaning Bede draws out from the text. But to give each phrase of the whole of Samuel a Christological meaning was a sustained and unparalleled effort. Through the text of this work Bede built up a complete book of instruction in doctrine and conduct for contemporary Christians.

In addition to the commentary and the list of names, Bede's other comments on the books of Samuel and Kings appeared in his answers to 30 questions posed to him by Nothelm, his colleague in London. These were 30 points arising out of each of the four books and concerned the literal meaning of the texts more than their spiritual interpretation. Bede asserted that in his replies he was 'following in the footsteps of the fathers', the chief of whom appears to have been Jerome, but as always, his own interests were included in his work. When for instance, he replied to a question about 2 Kings 20:9–10, 'Shall the shadow go forward ten steps or back ten steps?', he gave an explanation of the behaviour of shadows at the poles of the earth. He concludes with an exhortation addressed to 'the reader' perhaps indicating others beyond Nothelm:

> I pray the reader, if there is anything good in the explanations
> I have given, give praise for the gifts of God.[59]

Commentary on Genesis

The book of Genesis provided material especially congenial to Bede. In the well-stocked library at Jarrow he found commentaries of the early Fathers Basil, Ambrose, Jerome and Augustine on the accounts in Genesis of the days of the creation of the world in which they drew out from the text a doctrine of the creation of the natural world and of man's place within it. Here he found traces of the natural science of the ancient world, and here also the beginning of history with the expulsion of Adam and Eve from the eternal zone of paradise into the world of flux and change. The commentary therefore was both akin to Bede's earlier scientific treatises and provided a part of his plan for the ages of history which underlay so much of his work. In Genesis he found the texts vital to the discussion of creation, the Fall, and the promises of redemption.[60]

Bede's commentary on Genesis drew heavily on his predecessors. It seems probable that the first section of what is now the first book of his work had been compiled over some years (before 725) from extracts from these commentaries on the six days of creation, which he then used and expanded, adding a more hastily done section to bring the commentary up to the expulsion of Adam from paradise before sending it to Acca with a dedicatory letter. Later he returned to Genesis and added four books bringing the commentary up to the birth of Isaac and the expulsion of Ishmael. Commentary was given on each verse or group of verses of Genesis and Bede began with a collation of patristic commentaries on the text, as requested. He said as much in the accompanying letter to Bishop Acca:

> Nor was I dilatory in following out what you deigned to command, but rather at once after I had gone through the patristic volumes I gathered together from them and arranged in two books that which might form complete instruction for the unlearned reader, while the learned reader might use the gathering to ascend to higher and stronger advanced reading.[61]

In the commentary on Genesis he presented agreed insight into major topics of doctrine, whether culled from the past or from his own thoughts, to new Christians for their salvation. He had already found to his cost that originality could prove a minus rather than a plus, but this did not prevent him from restructuring the texts he used and adding more, especially in the way of 'higher and stronger' spiritual insights. As with the commentaries on the New Testament, it is in his use of the Fathers in combination with his own insights that Bede's originality lies. Some of the speculations of the Fathers he omitted entirely, for instance, the discussion by Ambrose at the beginning of Genesis of Plato, Aristotle and Pythagoras; and he replaced a personal comment by the Mediterranean-born Ambrose with his own reflections in a different climate:

> It is clear from these words of God that in the springtime the ordering and adornment of the world is perfected.[62]

Other comments are his alone; for instance, when discussing the name 'Adam', Bede used his skills in grammar and in two ancient languages as well as his sense of numerology and the wholeness of scripture to give a brilliant exposition:

> The name Adam contains four letters: 'a', 'd', 'a', 'm' and from these four letters the four quarters of the earth take their beginning when they are named in Greek. Among the Greeks the east is called *A natole*, the west *D isis*, the north *A rctos*, and the south *M esembria*. It is very right that the name of the first man, by whose progeny the whole world was to be filled, should contain mystically within itself all the four quarters of the world.[63]

The commentary on Genesis contains a carefully constructed account of the creation of the world, the Fall of man, his expulsion from paradise, the flood, the New Covenant with Abraham, and ends with the expulsion of Ishmael and the acceptance of Isaac, for many reasons a crucial point for Bede. The names of places and people were analysed and some linguistic points examined in detail, with reference to the old Latin, Greek and Hebrew (i.e. Jerome's Latin version of the Hebrew) texts. Other parts of the Scriptures were introduced to elucidate the narrative, and always the theme of Christ was drawn out of the text. For instance, in commenting on Genesis 14, the capture of Lot and his release by Abraham, Bede gave detailed explanations of each name and each place, taken from either Josephus or Jerome or both; then he used the numbers given to discover deeper significance in the story. The 'four kings with five' who took Lot captive signified for Bede, as for other patristic writers, the four elements of the world and the five senses; the 318 men released by Abraham along with Lot signified 'the most victorious cross and the name of our salvation' since, he says,

> in Greek 30 is represented by the Tau, which is the cross . . . ten and eight are the I and H, the first letters of the name of Jesus.[64]

Since Lot was captured by 'four kings with five', he signifies man taken captive by four elements and five senses and set free by the cross of Christ. Bede goes further and says,

> Abraham is the mystical figure of Christ, who by his passion and death redeemed the world from death in battle against the devil.[65]

In the last chapter of his commentary, on the expulsion of Ishmael and the acceptance of Isaac, Bede was able to use the commentary of Paul in his letter to the Galatians on this text, 'Abraham had two sons, one by a slave and one by a free woman' (Galatians 4:21–28) to justify his own interpretation. It was an especially appropriate section of Paul since it was the best of all authorities for the kind of understanding of the Scriptures which Bede was proposing. In a catena of New Testament texts, Bede expounded the doctrine of the two covenants under the image of the two sons of Abraham, so that the distinction between 'sons of the flesh' and 'sons of promise' was made both credible and immediate. Whatever may be thought of such use of the Old Testament, it had the authority of Paul behind it. And for an Anglo-Saxon preacher, faced with accounts of the strange behaviour of the old people of God, it was certainly more interesting and useful to discover in their conduct insights into the working of Providence that he could explain to his people than if Bede had remained with the 'historical' sense.

Though the main point of the commentary for Bede was a theological one and his intention in writing it pastoral, for later readers with different interests, there are also in this, as in other commentaries, sections which reflect the life and times of eighth-century England in a practical way. Bede knew of the building of Wearmouth by hearsay from those monks who had taken part in the foundation in 674 when he himself was an infant of two. The accounts of glaziers, stonecutters, builders in the Roman style were part of the history of his first monastery and when he was transferred to the new foundation of Jarrow, it seems more than likely that he both observed and took part in the building of the new monastery of St Paul. In the commentary on Genesis, this experience may be reflected in a passage describing bitumen, a glue mentioned in Scripture for the buildings in Babylon. Bede contrasts it with the cement used in his day for stonework:

> In wholesome contrast with this, we read that the temple of the Lord was made with cement. For cement is made from stones which have been burnt and turned to ash. These stones which were previously strong and firm, each one by itself, are worked upon by fire in such a way that when they have been softened by the addition of heat and when they have been joined together in a better way, they are themselves able to bind other stones which have been placed in position in the wall.[66]

He draws another moral from the process of building in stone which also suggests observation:

> When we are building a house, we begin the work by preparing our material and after this beginning we dig deeply. Next we put stones upon this foundation and then we place walls upon it in rising courses of stones, and so little by little we reach completion in the task upon which we have set out.[67]

In the commentary on the Song of Songs, likewise, there is a passage when he comments on the 'lattice' by describing lathe-work with the true enthusiasm of an observer, perhaps again a reflection of his attention as a boy to the workmen in his monastery.

But these were never just descriptions added to the text for their own sake: from observation as much as from words Bede drew meaning for the soul, especially about unity and peace. In his two homilies for the feast of the dedication of St Paul's, Jarrow, which took place 23 April 684/5 and of which the dedication stone still exists, Bede pursued the same theme, of the building up of the 'house of God' not only by solid stones but by the unity and perfection of the 'living stones' of the brothers' lives.

Commentaries on Ezra and Nehemiah, the Temple and the Tabernacle

In his commentaries on Ezra and Nehemiah, which he abandoned the text of Genesis to complete, and in his commentaries on both the description of the Temple in Kings 5:1 – 7:51 and the Tabernacle in Exodus 24:12 – 30:21, Bede's interest in the image of building and decorating churches was again prominent. The commentary on Ezra and Nehemiah is listed in the *Ecclesiastical History*, where it is also described as being in two books. It is also mentioned in *De Temporum Ratione* as an allegorical study:

> The outer context of the letter being stripped away, another and more sacred spiritual meaning is found in the kernel.[68]

This, together with the reference to it in the letter to Acca already quoted, suggests that this commentary was written between 725 and 732. Two other commentaries seem to belong to this period and have the same design of expounding the nature of the Church. In 'The tabernacle, its vessels and the priestly vestments: three books', which was written before the commentary on Mark, Bede expounded verses from Exodus 24:12 – 30:21 in relation to the Church and the Christian soul, and his treatise 'On the building of

the Temple, an allegorical interpretation like the others: two books'
was constructed on the same lines.

In all these three commentaries, the image of building and
rebuilding is examined to illustrate the realities of 'building spiritu-
ally'. There are notes on names, places, and objects, but the main
interest of the works, for Bede and for his readers, was not there.
Here Bede had no predecessor and with his already keen insight into
the significance of buildings, he at once used the texts which related
to the building of the Temple as signifying the interior work of
building up the body of Christ which is the Church. Each commentary is an intricate discussion of Christ and the Christian life:

> The house of God which King Solomon built in Jerusalem was
> made as a figure of the holy universal church which from its
> first election to its end is growing daily towards that end by the
> grace of the King; it is being built up in his peace which is
> redemption; a part of it still in pilgrimage, a part already free
> from the hardships of pilgrimage and reigning with him already
> in heaven.

Christ, he adds,

> is made the temple of God in assuming humanity and we are
> made into the temple of God by his spirit dwelling in us.[69]

After all his exposition in Genesis of the fallen state of man and the
necessity for redemption, Bede here discusses the practical ways in
which the salvation already completed by Christ can be activated in
the life of each Christian. In order to become a stone in this building,
each must be joined by the sacramental life of the Church to Christ,
by baptism entering into the fellowship of the Church, present and
departed. Thereafter, it is a matter of steady perseverance:

> After establishing the rudiments of the faith, after laying the
> foundations of humility in ourselves by following the example
> of holier men, a wall of good works must be raised on high, like
> courses of stones laid one upon another, by walking and
> advancing from virtue to virtue.[70]

For Bede the virtues of peace and unity were the cement in these
walls, which were not only a temple, a city, a tabernacle, but a
country:

> That supernal country where the eyes of the saints behold
> Christ the King in his beauty . . . love alone reigns.[71]

Bede followed Gregory the Great in his concern with pastoral matters, but Augustine in this vision of the Church in pilgrimage and in heaven.[72] The ideal of the two cities, inextricably intertwined until the end of all things, the completing of the City of God, fills these treatises.

Commentaries on Tobit, Proverbs, the Song of Songs and the Canticle of Habakkuk

If doctrinal matters formed the core of Bede's comments on Samuel and Genesis, and pastoral concern was the theme of the three treatises just mentioned, in his commentaries on other books of the Bible — Tobit, Proverbs, the Song of Songs and the Canticle of Habakkuk — Bede explored in a sustained way and with great delicacy the spiritual and mystical meaning beneath the letter, relating it to Christ and to the soul of each reader.

The commentary on 'the book of the blessed father Tobias' Bede described as 'an allegorical explanation concerning Christ and the Church'. It does not have a covering letter and may not have been done in answer to a request but out of Bede's own choice. In the first paragraph, he describes his work as an allegory in which the participants in the story are seen as symbolizing either the Jews, faithful to their religion while among Gentiles, the pagans under the domination of the devil, or Christ and the Church. The book of Tobit is a story about a journey, an image very much to Bede's mind, and the whole story is ruthlessly allegorized into the journey of faith from the old Israel to the new; even the dog is a sign for a preacher. Each verse is commented upon, and other parts of Scripture are used to elucidate a meaning both doctrinal and pastoral. The Jews were signified by Tobit, who went out faithfully to bury the dead but was blinded and unable to see truly; Tobias was a type of the Christian, led by the angel Raphael, whose name means 'the healing of God'. Together, they encountered many adventures, like preachers travelling among the heathen, in order that Tobias might meet Sara, a type of the Gentiles who were under the domination of the devil. By becoming the bride of Tobias, Sara was set free from the devils who had possessed her; together, they returned to Tobit, the Jewish people, and the old man recovered his sight, just as the veil of unbelief would be taken away from Israel:

> So after seven days, granted sight by Tobias, the wife of his
> son was brought to him [Tobit], because when through faith
> the eyes of the Jews have been opened, after that they receive

the grace of the Holy Spirit when the church is led to them, so that there may be one fold and one shepherd, and so that Christ may be the one cornerstone of the house.[73]

In commenting on the book of Proverbs, Bede believed them to come, like the Song of Songs, from King Solomon and treated it in a similar manner. He listed it as 'the works on the Proverbs of Solomon: in three books' and had completed it by 731. There is a copy of the Latin text of Proverbs (MS Bodley 819) which Lowe has identified as a Jarrow manuscript, possibly that used by Bede.

Bede did not leave even this very practical piece of advice on conduct as just that; the verses were given a spiritual significance about Christ and his Church. Bede begins by stating that he wanted to think of the Greek word *parabolas* and its Latin translation as *similitudines* as encouraging an allegorical interpretation. The speaker of the words, Solomon, the prince of peace, was for Bede a type of Christ, here advising the Christian soul. Every verse was therefore interpreted in this way; even the virtuous woman, whom one might have expected Bede to use as a model for womanly conduct, is allegorized as a type of the Church.

Bede's list of his works included 'On the Song of Songs: seven books', a work written over many years but complete by 731. Of these four treatises, the longest and by far the most important was this commentary on the Song of Songs, 'this book most difficult to understand'. In all his commentaries, including his first, Bede very frequently cited the Song of Songs, and indicated its spiritual meaning. His commentary is a superb work of mystical theology, a part of the rich tradition of Christian spiritual commentary on the text, where he was preceded by, for instance, Origen, Gregory of Nyssa, Ambrose, Tyconius, Gregory the Great and the Donatist Julian of Eclanum. It does not seem that Bede knew any of the earlier commentators, except Origen and Julian; the commentary of Gregory the Great may have reached him only when he had completed his work. Bede's commentary was much fuller than those of his predecessors, subtle and detailed, and in a Latin markedly more sophisticated than some of his earlier commentaries. It is a work of profound meditation on the mystery of Christ and the Church, unequalled until the twelfth century.

As Bede said in his account of poetry, drama was also to be found in the Bible, and he had cited there the Song of Songs as an example of poetic drama. In the commentary, he first set out the text as a play with lines for Christ, the Church and the Synagogue before beginning his analysis of each verse. The first book, composed last, was against the errors of Julian of Eclanum, whom Bede had quoted extensively and without realizing his status as a heretic. He found out too late that Julian had been condemned for his views on grace, in which he had adopted a Pelagian stance and opposed the view that all men were born in iniquity and were capable of transformation only by receiving the grace of God and not otherwise. Bede had read his *De Bono Constantiae*, and *De Institutione Virginis*, thinking them to have been by Jerome, but had later realized their heretical trend. He therefore wrote warning others of dangers in these texts and lamenting the isolation from the world of Christian theology which had laid him open to this error:

> Having been born and bred far outside the world, that is in an island of the ocean, we can only know of things that go on in the first places of the world, i.e. Arabia and India, Judea and Egypt, through the writings of those who have lived there.

The sixth book of Bede's commentary is a collection of extracts from the works of Gregory the Great, though not from his treatise on the same text. It is possible that Bede had collected these extracts over several years and used them as the basis for his own meditations. Bede's main commentary, however, is contained in Books 1 to 5.

The language of the Song of Songs has been consistently interpreted, by both Jews and Christians, in a mystical vein and in Bede's commentary this tradition reached a new height of excellence. He explicitly excluded an interpretation which would allow Mary the Mother of God a part in the dialogue:

> Where it is said, oh that you were nursed at my mother's breasts, I do not understand that to mean specially those of the glorious mother of God ... but the synagogue which is human nature from which was born the Redeemer of all.[74]

Using the persons of the bride, the bridegroom and the Synagogue, he commented verse by verse on the whole book, giving it meaning as a mystical song between Christ and redeemed humanity. He used the first person, singular and plural, and each verse evoked not just a sentence but at least a paragraph, often several pages of comment, and always with the same theme:

> Under the image of the bride and bridegroom, he [Solomon] speaks of the church and Christ, the eternal king and his city.[75]

As in the commentary on the book of Tobit, Bede saw the Jewish nation as vital in the history of salvation. The Church was here presented as drawing its existence from the Synagogue: it was the Synagogue which was 'black but comely', and first 'desired the Lord to come in the flesh'; it was to the Synagogue also that Bede assigned the verse 'Let him kiss me with the kisses of his mouth'.

In this commentary, Bede understood the text from the point of view of doctrine. Often the first interpretation of a phrase was in connection with the doctrine of the Trinity and only after that with the incarnate Christ and the Church. For instance, when commenting on the verse 'when I should find thee without, I would kiss thee' (Song of Songs 8:1) Bede says

> Within he is beloved: because in the beginning was the Word and the Word was with God and the Word was God. But when he came outside was when the Word was made flesh and dwelt among us. For the patriarchs and prophets saw the Lord, but within, that is, in spiritual contemplation of mind, not with the eyes of the flesh.[76]

The treatise, however, was for the use of preachers as well as the meditations of monks, and again and again Bede drew from the text lessons useful to the pastors of the flock: they were to be like palm trees, rich with fruit, growing out of the rough base of this world; they must have dove's eyes, which look only with love and simplicity; honey should be under their tongue so that they speak not out of vanity but out of a deep and humble heart.

At the end of his commentary on another work, Bede again returned to the image of the bride in the Song of Songs. This was his treatise 'On the Song of Habakkuk: one book'. This piece was Bede's only direct commentary on a text used regularly in the Office, with the exception of his homily on the Magnificat. It was the only work written for a woman and was addressed to 'my dearest sister', presumably abbess of one of the northern convents, perhaps Whitby or Coldingham, with whom Bede had corresponded to obtain material which he included in the *Ecclesiastical History*. The verses from Habakkuk 3:2–19 were recited each ferial Friday after the psalms at Lauds from an early period. This usage was familiar to Bede, suggesting that he knew it from his own monastery. It was a canticle peculiarly suitable for Fridays, the day celebrating the passion of Christ, a fact to which Bede refers. In the Eastern Church, a mystical commentary, phrased in Christian poetry, emerged from this text and replaced it in the Office of Dawn

(Orthros). Bede's reflections on the text follow similar lines. He commented verse by verse, and drew out of the text

> The mysteries of the Lord's Passion, Incarnation, Resurrection, Ascension, the spreading of faith of Gentiles and the rejection of Jews.[77]

It is a detailed and very beautiful analysis of the inner meaning of the words, seeing through them the mysteries of the death and resurrection of Christ in relation to the person singing them.

BEDE'S BIBLICAL TEACHING

In all his commentaries, doctrinal and philosophical speculations were never Bede's concern for their own sake. When given the opportunity for speculation, for instance, by the word 'God' in Genesis, he had little new to say about the nature of divinity and in commenting on the transfiguration of Christ in Mark's gospel, he did not dwell on it as a revelation of the Trinity, but explained it as a text closely related to other parts of Scripture, revealing the nature of the person of Christ and the hope this gives to the believer. But he was no dull or mundane thinker; there is always in his writings a sense of urgency, of longing and desire for the presence of Christ in the England of his own times. When he spoke of the Eucharist it was as a manifestation of Christ in the present among his people; when he wrote about Christian life, it was always as a pilgrimage towards the homeland of heaven, for those alive and in England, and above all, the study of the Scriptures was for Bede a matter of the utmost seriousness and urgency.

In the *Letter to Egbert*, Bede expressed his anxiety about those Christian contemporaries who were less than careful about their faith. He exclaimed against the preferences of even bishops for 'laughing, joking, story telling, feasting and drinking' instead of 'feeding their souls with heavenly sacrifices'.[78] Such deviations from the direct route of the pilgrim passing through this world to 'the perpetual vision of the Godhead among the choir of angels' were weaknesses to be reproved and changed. What he saw with a more severe eye was deliberate laziness in those who were committed to teaching the Gospel and in those who had heard it from them. Teachers were urgently needed, not a leisured and highly instructed priestly caste but spiritual people who would 'hear the word of God and keep it' in good lives. He condemned those who acquired learning of the Scriptures for their own glory, as much as he disapproved of heretics and despised pagans. For Bede Christianity was a matter of the utmost seriousness and as a consequence, while it offered rewards beyond thought, it involved also the risk of infinite loss. He did not shrink from commenting on passages of Scripture about death and judgement, while the dreams of Drythelm and Fursa with their insight into both options after death occupied important pages in the *Ecclesiastical History*:

> At the day of judgement, when all the glory of the world is perishing and there remains to the ungodly only the presence of their past life, they shall say, 'What has pride profited us? Or what has the vaunting of riches brought us? All these things are passed away as a shadow.'[79]

But Bede had no simplistic categories of those who can be known to be saved or damned. Shaken by his own experience of a monk dying without repentance for sin in his own monastery, Bede never held sin lightly, but he was not naïve about identifying sinners:

> Our works and words, no doubt, may be known to men. But with what intention they are accomplished and where we desire to go by their means, He alone knows who sees what each thinks and in what he takes delight.[80]

In order to give the new English preachers the resources for their solemn task, Bede turned all his abilities and his knowledge of languages, geography, natural science, numerology, and cosmology, as well as his vast reading in the various books of the Fathers, to provide his contemporaries with tools for conversion, for themselves and for others. He was always eager to make clear the literal, grammatical and historical meaning of a text, though what the text had meant in its original setting was of virtually no interest to him or his readers. In his commentaries, especially those on the Old Testament, there is a kind of wondering delight as he uncovers the whole story of redemption from every page of the Scriptures, and presents it as the only food for wayfaring men. Using images derived from the kitchen, he summed up the way in which he and his readers were to feed upon the Word of God in the Scriptures:

> We are being fed on food roasted on a gridiron when we understand literally, openly and without any covering the things that have been said or done to protect the health of the soul; upon food cooked in a frying pan when by frequent

turning over of the superficial meaning and by looking at it afresh we comprehend what there is in it that corresponds allegorically with the mysteries of Christ, what with the condition of the catholic church and what with setting right the ways of individuals. Afterwards we search the oven for the bread of the Word when by exertion of mind we lay hold of those mystical meanings in the Scriptures, that is, upon matters concealed aloft which as yet we cannot see but which we hope to see in the future.[81]

It was this single-minded search for the 'bread of the Word' which informed all his commentaries.

Bede's learning was not a secret for himself alone. His brothers, colleagues, pupils and friends were eager to share in the riches he uncovered and which filled him with delight. His reading was 'for my own benefit' but also 'for that of my brothers', and the letters which preface many of the commentaries through which he shared his own understanding with them also show that it was monastic and indeed clerical readers beyond his own monastery that he had in mind. It seems that others asked him to teach them through writing. There is, of course, a convention of humility, which caused any ancient and mediaeval writer to protest that he only wrote because urged to do so, but with Bede this seems to have had reality: the letters of Bishop Acca and others are not only stylized prefaces but also genuine responses to situations and show the kind of pressure his friends put upon him to write and publish. He wrote in Latin, and therefore he wrote for a relatively small audience in England, though outside England in place and in time he wrote in an international language which was far more available than Anglo-Saxon. Bede's didactic works were for present and immediate use, the historical works preserved the past, the commentaries were to communicate the wisdom of the past to the present but in fact also preserved the past for the future. While his didactic works were a part of the classroom for the Anglo-Saxon beginners in front of him and, as he says, needed the presence of a teacher, and the *Ecclesiastical History* was directed to a secular audience who were interested in the past of the English, the commentaries were part of a longer and wider tradition.

Bede's commentaries placed him among the Doctors of the universal Church, but they were written with an immediate and practical end in view. Bede himself loved reading and could not have enough of it but he knew that the clergy of England had neither the time nor the opportunity given him and had less zeal for learning, as he said in a letter to Bishop Acca:

> The volumes [of the Fathers] are so numerous and so large that only the very rich could acquire them; they are so deep that they can only be read by the most learned.

Such volumes of the Fathers were not self-explanatory; it was necessary to clarify as well as transmit:

> Not all the works of the Fathers are in everyone's hands and many readers are ignorant of scriptural problems, not because they have not been explained by the doctors of the church but because either they do not have them or if they do have them they have not understood them.

Bede says he has therefore

> gone through the books of the fathers and collected from them whatever can instruct the untrained reader.[82]

Bede's commentaries on the Scriptures were meant first of all for the devout, especially monks and nuns. The allegorical interpretations of the Scriptures were well-known to monks by constant repetition in church or private reading for prayer, and Bede's expositions of them were therefore particularly useful for religious who wanted to go deeper into the texts they used constantly, but the audience chiefly in Bede's mind was the clergy. He sent most of his commentaries to a bishop, Acca of Hexham, a man of learning, a close friend of Bede, and one constantly involved in the affairs of a diocese. They were meant for those whose work was preaching and teaching and as such they formed a part of the missionary, evangelical work of the times, so that the new converts should receive from their clergy true and apostolic teaching. In his last work, the *Letter to Egbert*, his former pupil, later archbishop of York, the full concern of Bede with the clergy and their responsibility to preach and teach truly is manifest, but it also underlies the text of all the commentaries:

> The shepherds did not conceal in silence the hidden mysteries which they had learned from God but declared them to whoever they could. This was because the spiritual shepherds of the church are chiefly ordained to this end: to preach the mysteries of the word of God and to show the wonderful things they have learned in Scripture to the admiration of their hearers.[83]

Articulate people, especially those consecrated to communicating the word of the Gospel to the English, were constantly in Bede's mind; he was one with them as a priest, and fulfilled his own commission to preach the word by teaching the teachers, but it was not the official clergy only that he had in mind. There was a duty of exposition and therefore of learning for every Christian who was responsible for others, a kind of spiritual qualification for preaching:

> But by shepherds we must understand here not only bishops, priests and deacons or even monastic superiors, but all the faithful however small their house may be are rightly called shepherds insofar as they rule over that house with watchful care.[84]

He even proposed, tentatively, that a slave would be better off in such a household than free:

> he may be more honestly and piously educated and governed than if taken into freedom.[85]

To be able to guide others rightly, such 'shepherds' needed themselves to be fed and guided, especially among the more mysterious parts of the Scriptures, where allegory was the gateway into the 'faith that works by love'. But this was not to say that he saw the text of the Scriptures as the perquisite of an elect and literate few; he knew very well that the English were reluctant to learn Latin and often deplored it though not in a defeatist way; with the lament came the remedy:

> I have planned to take into account the inertia of our nation, that is the English, which not so long since, that is in the time of Pope Gregory the Great, received the seed of faith and has cherished it only lukewarmly so far as reading is concerned. I have decided not only to elucidate the meaning but also to compress the arguments. For clear brevity is usually better for memorizing than prolix argument.[86]

It was to Bede a duty for all to know the Scriptures, including the Old Testament, at least through hearing if not through sight:

> For if Moses and all the prophets spake of Christ and hence how he entered by his bitter passion into his glory, what reason have they to glory in being Christians who according to the measure of their strength neither desire to investigate how the Scriptures relate to Christ nor to attain through suffering tribulation to the glory which they want to have in Christ?[87]

The understanding of Scripture was for Bede hard work:

> We must apply ourselves continually lest those things which
> have been written for us (1 Corinthians 10:11) escape us
> because of our torpor or laziness.[88]

He adds elsewhere:

> he is dumb who does not understand that a spiritual meaning
> is present in the letters.[89]

Though Bede urged the closest possible attention to learning, in this
area, even more than in his other skills, he was not in any way an
intellectual snob; those who were responsible for preaching must
learn to their maximum capacity but for those who could not, there
were other ways to understanding. His pleasure in the paintings
imported by Benedict Biscop to Jarrow was neither aesthetic nor
exclusive but was caused by the fact that they made evangelical
truth more available to the non-reading people:

> Thus all who entered the church, even those who could not
> read, were able, whichever way they looked, to contemplate
> the dear face of Christ and his saints even if only in a picture,
> and put themselves more firmly in mind of the Lord's Incar-
> nation, and as they saw the decisive moment of the Last
> Judgement before their very eyes be brought to examine their
> conscience with all due severity.[90]

The fact that at the end of his life he was ready to consider
translation into the newly written English language was a part of
this pastoral approach to the Scriptures. He had no time for
learning for learning's sake, just as he had little to say in favour of
reading of literature other than Christian:

> Better is a stupid and unlettered brother who, working the
> good things he knows, merits life in heaven than one who
> though being distinguished for his learning in the scriptures,
> or even holding the place of a doctor, lacks the bread of love.[91]

His commentaries were not antiquarian pieces but pastoral in intent
and offered as immediately useful to the reader. The whole of the
Bible was for Bede filled with Christ and his work as commentator
was to make this available to others. He did not see Christianity as
an intellectual game for an élite; it was about facts and events and
people, and it was meant for all. Mere apprehension of meaning was

not the end of Christian learning. In commenting on the 'morning star' in 2 Peter he says,

> What is the morning star? If you say the Lord, it is too little. The morning star is our own excellent understanding. For if this arises in our hearts it will be enlightened, it will be made clear. It will become love such as we now wish and long for yet do not possess and we shall see of what sort it will be in each other just as now we see each other's faces.[92]

Notes

1 HA, 6 and 9.

2 *Life of Ceolfrith, Abbot of the Monastery at Wearmouth and Jarrow*, ed. and trans. D. S. Boutflower (London, 1912), 20, p. 69. For discussion of the *Codex Amiatinus* see R. L. S. Bruce Mitford, *The Art of the Codex Amiatinus* (Jarrow Lecture, 1967).

3 Bede's text of the Bible is discussed in M. L. W. Laistner, 'The library of the Venerable Bede' in BLTW, pp. 237-66. For an illuminating discussion of the text *not* used by Bede for Revelation, see H. Sparks, 'Bede's text of the Apocalypse', *Journal of Theological Studies*, new series, 5.2 (1954), pp. 227-31.

4 M. L. W. Laistner, Introduction to and edition of *Acts*. See also M. L. W. Laistner, 'The Latin version of Acts known to Bede', *Transactions of the Royal Historical Society* (1937), pp. 37-50, for Bede's use of *Codex Laudianus Graecus* (MS Bodley 35).

5 *Luke* 11:14, p. 231.

6 *Collectio Psalterii Bedae* in *Homilies*, pp. 452-70.

7 '*Seduli Patrum vestigia sequentes*': *Song of Songs*, p. 180.

8 For discussion of the library at Jarrow see M. L. W. Laistner, 'The library of the Venerable Bede', op. cit.

9 *Acts* (R) 11:6, p. 99.

10 *Luke*, p. 7, Letter to Acca. The source marks are reproduced in the CCSL edition of *Luke* and *Mark*. Cf. M. L. W. Laistner, 'Source marks in Bede MSS', *Journal of Theological Studies* 34 (1933), pp. 350-4; E. J. Sutcliffe, 'Quotations in the Venerable Bede's commentary on Mark', *Biblica* 7 (1926), pp. 428-39.

11 HA (Farmer), 6, pp. 190-1.

12 Ibid., 9, p. 194.

13 *Homilies* I, 14, p. 100.

14 Augustine, *On Christian Doctrine* 11.viii.

15 *Tabernacle*, p. 65.

16 *Luke*, Prologue, p. 7.

17 *Revelation*, Letter to Hwaetberht, col. 134.

18 *Tabernacle* 1, pp. 24–5.

19 *Revelation*, Preface, col. 131. For an excellent discussion of this topic, cf. Gerald Bonner, *St Bede in the Tradition of Western Apocalyptic Commentary* (Jarrow Lecture, 1966).

20 *Homilies* II, 13, p. 269. For discussion of the allegorical sense of Scripture and Bede, see Henri de Lubac SJ, *Exégèse médiévale: les quatre sens de l'Ecriture* I (Paris, 1959), pp. 142–6.

21 The collection of Bede's extracts from Augustine on Paul has never been edited; for list of surviving MSS see A. Wilmart, *Revue Bénédictine* XXXVIII (1926), pp. 16–52. For a full account of the surviving manuscripts of all Bede's works, see M. L. W. Laistner, *A Handlist of Bede Manuscripts* (New York, 1943).

22 *Acts*, Letter to Acca, p. 4.

23 *Epistles: Commentary on 1 John* 1:1, p. x.

24 *Revelation*, Preface, col. 129.

25 Ibid., col. 131.

26 Ibid., col. 144.

27 *Luke*, Prologue, p. 10.

28 *Revelation* 6:8, col. 376 (Marshall, p. 36).

29 Ibid., 4:8, col. 144 (Marshall, p. 33).

30 Augustine, *On the Psalms*, Psalm 149:4(3).

31 Revelation 5:8, col. 173.

32 Ibid., 2:23, col. 140.

33 Ibid., 21:19, col. 203. Cf. also Chapter 2, p. 35.

34 Ibid., 14:13, col. 175.

35 *Epistles* (Hurst): *Commentary on 1 Peter* 2:5, p. 83.

36 Ibid., *1 Peter* 1, p. 69.

37 Ibid., *1 Peter* 5:2, p. 114.

38 Ibid., *1 Peter* 2:1, p. 134.

39 Ibid., *1 Peter* 3:7, p. 96.

40 *Luke* 17:29, p. 330.

41 *Genesis* 1:28, p. 28.

42 *Homilies* II, 7, p. 230.

43 *Acts* 1:3, p. 6.

44 *Acts*(R), Preface, p. 93; cf. discussion by C. Jenkins, 'Bede as exegete and theologian' in BLTW, pp. 152–200; and P. Meyvaert, 'Bede the scholar' in *Famulus Christi*, pp. 40–69.

45 *Acts*(R) 6:8, p. 108. Trans. C. Jenkins in BLTW, pp. 157–8.

46 HE, V:15, p. 509.

47 *Homilies* II, 14, p. 275.

48 Ibid., p. 276.

49 *Luke* 24:53, pp. 424–5.

50 *Mark* 9:29, p. 550.

51 *Homilies* II, 14, p. 279.

52 Ibid., II, 8, p. 275.

53 Ibid., II, 9, p. 240.

54 Ibid.

55 Cf. Judith McClure, 'Bede's Old Testament Kings' in *Ideal and Reality in Frankish and Anglo-Saxon Society*, ed. P. Wormald, D. Bullough and R. Collins (Oxford, 1983), pp. 76–99.

56 *Ezra and Nehemiah* 3:19, p. 352.

57 *Samuel* 3:6, p. 36.

58 Ibid., Prologue, p. 9.

59 Ibid., Question 30, p. 322.

60 For discussion of the text of Bede on Genesis, see Judith McClure, 'Bede's *Notes on Genesis* and the training of the Anglo-Saxon clergy' in *The Bible in the Medieval World*, ed. K. Walsh and D. Wood (Oxford, 1985), pp. 17–31.

61 *Genesis*, Preface, p. 1.

62 Ibid., 1:11–13, p. 14.

63 Ibid., 5:2–3, p. 93; trans. P. Hunter Blair, *Northumbria in the Days of Bede* (London, 1976), p. 215.

64 Ibid., 14:14, p. 187.

65 Ibid.

66 Ibid., 1:8–9, p. 160; P. Hunter Blair, op. cit., p. 206.

67 Ibid., 1:1, p. 3; P. Hunter Blair, op. cit., p. 206.

68 DTR, p. 195.

69 *Ezra*, pp. 241–2.

70 Ibid.

71 *Temple*, p. 176.

72 Cf. Gerald Bonner, 'Bede and his legacy', *Durham University Journal* LXXVIII.2 (June 1986).

73 *Tobit* 9:18, p. 17.

74 *Song of Songs* 8:1, p. 338.

75 Ibid., 1:1, p. 190.

76 Ibid., 8:1, p. 338.

77 *Habakkuk* 1:1, p. 381.

78 *Letter to Egbert* (Whitelock), p. 737.

79 *Revelation* 18:9, col. 185 (Marshall, p. 123).

80 Ibid., 2:23, col. 139 (Marshall, p. 23).

81 *Samuel* 9:2-6, p. 87; trans. P. Hunter Blair, op. cit., p. 205.

82 *Genesis*, Preface, p. 1.

83 *Homilies* I, 7, p. 49.

84 Ibid.

85 *Luke* 6:30, p. 144.

86 *Revelation*, Preface, col. 74 (Marshall, pp. 8-9).

87 *Luke* 24:25-27, p. 415.

88 *Samuel*, Prologue, p. 9.

89 *Luke* 1:24, p. 29.

90 HA (Farmer), 6, pp. 190-1.

91 *Proverbs* 12:9, p. 76.

92 *1 Peter* 1:19, p. 132.

4

Bede and the saints

Christ is the morning star who when the night of this world is past will bring his saints to the promise of the light of life and everlasting day.[1]

Throughout his work on the Scriptures and on sacred history, Bede was concerned to present not only advice and instruction for pilgrims *in via* but also the encouragement of describing those already *in patria*, the stars of the new heaven. Hagiography has a central place in Bede's writings and it is not by accident that so great a part of his *Ecclesiastical History* is about saints. In his biblical commentaries and in his homilies also he turned again and again almost with relief to the holy ones in the Bible. With equal pleasure, he read accounts of sanctity in the patristic era, and wrote about two saints of the early Church, Felix and Anastasius. In his own time and place, he had also known saints or known those who had known them, whether in his own monastery or at Lindisfarne and elsewhere. His *History of the Abbots of Wearmouth–Jarrow* was written from the heart, while his lives of Cuthbert, in verse and prose, were among his most popular works. In his account of the Christianizing of the Anglo-Saxons, saints occupied much of the text. To Bede, as to Gregory the Great, saints were proof that the message of salvation actually worked in transforming real human beings into the likeness of Christ. In his accounts of saints he saw in them the life of Christ, manifest in signs and in miracles, while in the *History of the Abbots* he presented a central, unadorned, core of virtue which he had found in his friends.

BEDE AND HAGIOGRAPHY

In considering Bede's writings about the saints it is necessary to make a more general point about hagiography and distinguish between the hero and the holy one. The hagiographer has a different task and a different aim from the panegyrist or the biographer; hagiography is neither religious epic nor tentative biography but a different literary form. From the New Testament onwards there has been a way of describing Christian sanctity which is integral to its subject. It is not a pattern imposed later by others to distort the facts but a highlighting of those elements in the lives of certain people which made them saints. This pattern has been from the first century until today the life, death and resurrection of Jesus Christ. Christians are not called saints because they are interesting or brave, pious, just, well-behaved or great; they are saints insofar as they 'put on Christ' (Galatians 3:27), 'in whom dwells all the fulness of the Godhead' (Colossians 2:9). The result of this may well be that others then see in them such virtues; they may also experience through them that work of God which is called miracle. But the central concern of the saint is not to talk about life in Christ but to have it and the work of a hagiographer is to present this Christlikeness to others who run the same race, as model, as encouragement, and as assurance that they are surrounded by a great cloud of witnesses and that with God all things are possible. The question that Bede, like any hagiographer, asked is not: what school did this man go to? who were his friends and enemies? what were his hobbies? or what did he look like? but whether in this human life and death the marks of the Lord Jesus were visible. For Bede, the primary pattern for a saint's life was Christ and the primary literary pattern for him as a hagiographer was the Bible. In presenting the saints, he wrote in direct continuity with the tradition he found in the Bible and the early Church, bringing it up to his own time and indeed to his own abbey.

It is perfectly true that Bede's saints' lives contain material which is odd, non-factual, elusive. The accounts he worked from had often been told and retold, altered and combined or reduced; additions from folklore and popular imagination had crept in; but in the hands of a great historian and a great theologian, a master of both factual account and theological reality, the accounts of the saints attained a new value. On the one hand, Bede, like the New Testament writers, wrote as a careful historian, concerned with real people, convinced of the plain existence of his subjects. As an historian, he gives names, places and dates and describes his sources for his hagiographies with more care than for his accounts of other things, well aware that Christianity is about living people and is neither a myth, a philosophy nor a moral code. But on the other hand, he was also convinced that Christianity is not *only* about 'the historical Jesus' and hagiography not just about an earthly sequence of events. The New Testament writers had seen in the person of Jesus Christ an ultimate significance and Bede as a writer of saints' lives looked at his subjects in the same way. Their miracles were not to him *miracula*, wonders, but *signa*, signs of a greater reality and truth. Their lives were not interesting, either to Bede or his audience, as a reflection of life in the kingdom of Northumbria but as accounts of how life in that place had been lived orientated towards the kingdom of heaven. His works are full of a sense of longing for heaven, of life on earth as a pilgrimage, a vision of life in which all reality was placed on the other side of death:

> How do they long to gaze on Christ, whose face they never cease to behold, unless it is that the contemplation of the presence of God gives such joy to the citizens of heaven that in a way we cannot understand they are both satisfied at seeing his glory and always hungering for such sweetness as if it were always new.[2]

That bright promise lay ahead; the present world for Bede was full of risk for those who looked for salvation; it was the old age of the world, 'the old age of senility . . . to be consummated by the death of all the world' or, as Augustine had said, 'The world is passing away, the world is losing its grip, the world is short of breath'. In this life there was no certainty compared to the life of heaven:

> All the rest and hope and joy of the elect is only in the future sabbath where those who in this life walk with the Lord, humbly following his precepts, are taken up by him into the life of perpetual rest and do not again appear among mortals but live immortal with him.[3]

Such a conclusion of glory was not difficult to obtain; it was not reserved for an elect but open to the humblest and most ignorant; among the saints described in the *Ecclesiastical History* there were kings and thanes, queens and princesses, cowherds, married people, as well as priests and monks: anyone who persevered in following Christ could hope to become a part of that heaven:

We now sing the praises of his grace so that we may deserve to overcome and in the future never cease to sing them because we have overcome.[4]

The future glory was glimpsed even *in via* and in commenting on one of his favourite passages in the Bible, the account of the Transfiguration, Bede sees the glory of heaven already revealed on earth:

Oh how great is the perpetual felicity of the vision of God seen amid the choir of angels, if even the humanity of Christ and the society of two saints seen for a brief space was so delightful that Peter wished through satisfaction to stay there and not depart.[5]

SAINTS IN THE BIBLE

Bede's understanding of the saints in glory was not an idealistic fantasy of aloof perfection but a realistic apprehension of the life of human beings who had lived and died on earth and who now, already in the 'rest' of the seventh age, were vitally concerned in the life of those still in the sixth. This sense of the reality of the saints, as predecessors there and as witnesses still present here, underlies his comments when he writes about those saints mentioned in the Scriptures as having known Christ during his earthly life. He refers to the Virgin Mary in his commentaries on the gospels, and in several of his homilies, always both with a theologically precise appreciation of her place in the history of salvation and in a tone of love and veneration which is entirely personal. In a homily on the Magnificat, he says,

She has every right to rejoice in Jesus, that is in her Saviour, with greater joy than other saints, because she knew that she was going to give birth in course of time to the one whom she recognized as the eternal author of salvation. For He would truly be her son and her lord in one and the same person.[6]

In his commentary on the same passage in the gospel of Luke he makes the same point again, but this time by recasting the first phrase. 'My soul doth magnify the Lord', and expanding it in the first person, a literary form he rarely used and which is therefore the more striking as an example of the personal aspect of his devotion to Mary:

The Lord, she said, has exalted me with a great and unheard-of gift which cannot be explained in any words and can scarcely be understood by the feelings of the heart. And so I offer up all the strength of my soul in thanksgiving and praise. In my joy I pour out all my life, all my feeling, all my understanding in contemplating the greatness of him who is without end. My spirit rejoices in the eternal divinity of Jesus, my Saviour, whom I have conceived in time and bear in my body.[7]

Bede wrote about Mary with delight and sensitivity as a real person but this did not blur his theological understanding of her as one chosen to become Mother of God, and therefore as the second Eve:

Just as sin began from women so too it was fitting that blessings should spring from women and that life which was lost through the deception of one woman should be given back to the world by these two women [Mary and Elizabeth] who rival each other in giving praise.[8]

Moreover, he presents Mary in a very practical way in relation to the daily life of the monks of Jarrow as their source of peace and refreshment:

It has become an excellent and salutary custom in the church for everyone to sing this hymn [the Magnificat] daily in the Office of evening prayer. In this way the faithful, being reminded more often of the Incarnation of the Lord, are moved to devotion and also strengthened in virtue by the regular repetition of the remembrance of his mother's example. It is fitting that this should take place at evening prayer, for at the end of the day our minds are tired and prey to distractions and it is very useful to have this moment of quiet then to recollect ourselves and gather our thoughts.[9]

Bede is never fanciful about Mary, but understands her place in the gospels and refers to her in his homilies and commentaries with a warmth of feeling which would communicate her theological significance for the benefit of his readers and hearers. In his homily on the Purification, it was her humility which was stressed and recommended; in an Advent homily for the Annunciation, it was her receptivity which was presented as a pattern; and in a series of sermons for the Nativity, a feast for which he was himself above all responsible in his dating of the year, he brought all his understanding of the Bible and Fathers to bear upon the mystery of the Incarnation, linking each insight to the person of Mary:

> Let us with all the desire of our souls and casting aside all fleshly desires, cross over to that heavenly Bethlehem which is the house of the Living Bread so that him whom we now see lying weak in a manger we may deserve to look upon seated on the throne of the Father . . . The shepherds of the Lord's flock follow the lives of the Fathers who have gone before us, by, as it were, contemplating the gates of Bethlehem, in which this Bread of Life abides, and they find there nothing save the virginal beauty of the church, that is, Mary, the steadfast company of spiritual guides, that is, Joseph, and the humble birth of Christ lying between the pages of Sacred Scripture, that is, the infant lying in a manger.[10]

In his presentation of the other saints who, like Mary, had known Christ in his earthly life, that is, the apostles and others mentioned in the New Testament, Bede follows the same pattern. They are seen as holy because of their contact with Christ and they are therefore presented as encouragement and example to others. He paid special attention to Peter and Paul, the patrons of his own monastery, dwelling on the details about them in the gospels and in Acts, commenting on their writings in the New Testament. Peter especially was for Bede an example and a teacher as well as an intercessor. Moreover, the apostles were not only to be contacted through prayer and reading; when Benedict Biscop returned from Rome, Bede proudly recorded that he brought, next in value to Bede after the books, 'an abundant supply of relics of the blessed apostles and Christian martyrs which were to prove such a boon to many churches in the land'.[11] Hardly a page of the *Lives of the Abbots* is without some reference to St Peter, and in the *Ecclesiastical History* St Peter is the focus of pilgrimage to Rome, the severe rebuker of Archbishop Laurence, as well as the saint whose position as door-keeper of heaven turned the decision of Oswiu at the Council of Whitby. In a homily on the apostle, Bede used his favourite method of Scripture analysis to present Peter as the model of Christian faith: he began with a practical explanation of the city of Caesarea Philippi and a grammatical explanation of 'Bar-Jonah' as meaning 'son of a dove':

> For the dove is a very simple creature and Peter followed the Lord with a wise and good simplicity.

He added two other interpretations of 'dove' from other parts of Scripture:

> Mindful of the precept he with the other disciples had received from their Master, 'be ye therefore wise as serpents and simple as doves', and also because the Holy Spirit descended in the form of a dove, he is rightly called the 'son of a dove' because he showed that he was filled with spiritual grace.

The rest of the sermon was built round this concept of the faith and love of 'Peter, the son of the Holy Spirit', and after a careful exposition of Peter's affirmation of Christ as the Son of God, which Bede sees as an example of the doctrine of the Trinity, he urges his hearers, the brothers of his own monastery, not only to understand the mystery but to learn from it:

> Let us learn with all our hearts the mystery of the faith . . . and bring forth works worthy of that faith.

Nor is this the prosaic conclusion; in two final points, Bede introduces first a passage from the most mystical of all the books of Scripture, the Song of Songs (4:1):

> We also shall be called the sons of the dove . . . and Christ rejoicing in the spiritual increase of our souls will say to us: 'How beautiful thou art, my love, thou hast doves' eyes'.

He ended with a mosaic of Old and New Testament quotations:

> so shall it be to us who heap upon the rock of faith gold, silver and precious stones, that is, perfect works of virtue, the fires of tribulation shall bring no harm, no storm of temptation shall prevail against us, but rather made strong through trials we shall deserve to receive that crown of life which he promised to us before all ages, who with the Father in the unity of the Holy Ghost, lives and reigns God for ever and ever.[12]

Other biblical saints were also the focus of Bede's meditation and always with the same sense of friendship with them, the same care about doctrine and the same application of the inner meaning to be discerned through the text to those hearing or reading what he had to say. Of Matthew the publican he wrote:

> Not only did he prepare a banquet for the Lord in his home on earth but what was much more welcome to the Lord he made a feast in the house of his soul by faith and love, as is testified by him who said, 'Behold I stand at the door and knock; if any

one hears my voice and opens the door I will come in to him
and eat with him and he with me'.

Such an example was no mere matter for wonder; Bede at once
applied the text to those who were listening to his homily:

We open the door to the sound of his voice to receive him
when we freely assent to his promptings, whether secret or
open and when we do what we know we should do. He enters
then to eat with us and we with him since he lives in the hearts
of his elect by the gift of his love.[13]

THE SAINTS OF THE EARLY CHURCH

The festivals of such biblical saints formed the framework of the
liturgical year but the calendar contained commemorations of other,
later, saints. For Bede these others, at rest in the seventh age of the
world, were equally to be venerated. He praised the saints of the early
Church at various times, especially in his poem on Aethelthryth
(Etheldreda) of Ely, where he wove references to some early Christian
women martyrs into an elaborate pattern of praise, with the Anglo-
Saxon queen as their equal. It is a revealing list: first he mentions the
Virgin Mary, as 'head of the virgin-choir', then Agatha, a child
martyr connected with Rome, who was commemorated in a poem by
Venantius Fortunatus and to whom two churches in Rome had been
dedicated. The next to be praised was Eulalia, a Spanish child martyr
commemorated by Prudentius in a hymn and by Augustine in a sermon; then Thecla, the legendary companion of Paul, whose highly-
coloured story Bede, surprisingly, seems to have accepted in spite
of the doubts of both Tertullian and Jerome. Next in his list is
Euphemia, a child martyr of Chalcedon, in whose church the Council
of Chalcedon had been held in 451. She was commemorated by
Asterius of Arles in a panegyric and Pope Sergius (687–701) had
recently restored her church in Rome. The next two, Agnes and
Cecilia, were, like Agatha, young Roman martyrs, mentioned in the
Canon of the Mass; Agnes was praised by Prudentius, Ambrose and
Augustine, with a famous Roman basilica dedicated in her honour,
while Cecilia was also commemorated in a Roman church. All of
these were also mentioned by Bede in his martyrology, and it is certain
that he knew their alleged stories well. To such heroines of chastity
and faith he then added an elderly and married queen of Northumbria,
who died safely in her bed in 679:

> Nor lacks our age its Aethelthryth as well,
> its virgin wonderful.[14]

She was placed in this company on the evidence of her incorrupt body and the assertions of her confessor Wilfrid about her continued state of celibacy through two royal marriages. For this, Bede saw her as a virgin and associate of the Queen of heaven:

> Royal mother of heaven's King your leader now,
> You too may be a mother of heaven's King.

As elsewhere, Bede was affirming the sanctity of three states of life: that of the virgins, the married and the widows, but here they were also linked with the primary category of Christian sanctity, the martyrs. With all his appreciation of the state of virginity, Bede was no romantic; the martyr was one who had suffered with the Lord; the true virgin was one who followed the ascetic life of identification with the Cross:

> Whoever renounces marriage and consecrates their virginity to the Lord should manifest the behaviour suitable for virgins.[15]

Among later saints, Bede knew of Benedict of Nursia both through the *Dialogues* of Gregory the Great and through the *Rule of St Benedict*, which was among the seventeen rules which influenced his abbots in deciding about the way of life to be followed in the twin monasteries,[16] but there is no written account of him among Bede's works. It was the other Benedict, his first abbot, who received his praise, both in the *History of the Abbots* and in a homily. Alone of all Bede's homilies, this one was of local interest only; Paul the Deacon left it out of his collection of Bede's homilies, and replaced it with a sermon on Benedict of Nursia:

> The Venerable Bede in the last of his homilies, that is to say the fiftieth, treats almost exclusively of the life and deeds of a certain Benedict, a recluse in his monastery. Since this reading would be of no use in our Offices, I, Paul the Deacon, the least of the servants of Blessed Benedict, so that the number of fifty homilies should not be at all diminished, have composed with the help of grace from on high, this fiftieth homily for the glory of God and in honour of our most holy father Benedict.[17]

Bede might not praise Benedict directly but his biographer, Gregory the Great, was one of Bede's heroes. He called him 'the apostle of the English' and in the *Ecclesiastical History* he wrote a generous appreciation of one whom he revered as a Father of the Church and proudly claimed as the moving spirit in the evangelization of his country.

THREE SAINTS' LIVES

Twice more Bede wrote about saints of the early Church and in each case, as with his other account of a saint in the *Life of St Cuthbert*, he was rewriting, not composing: the *Life of St Anastasius* and the *Life of St Felix* were based on earlier accounts. In all three cases, Bede did not accept blindly what he has been given as a written text, but examined it, as he would a text of the Bible, in order to have a correct and valid account; then he held over it the lens of the Scriptures, in order to bring out of the text more clearly the theological meaning of the subject. The first necessity was to know what was written about a saint, and when he mentioned the life of Anastasius in his list of the books he had written, he expressed his dissatisfaction with the Latin text which had been translated from the Greek:

> A book on the life and passion of St Anastasius which was badly translated from the Greek by some ignorant person, which I have corrected as best I could to clarify the meaning.[18]

The Greek life of the Persian monk and martyr (d. 628) had been written two years after his death, when his body was translated to the monastery of St Sergius near Bethsaloe; in the mid-seventh century his head was venerated in Rome, which perhaps prompted a translation of his life into Latin. This version, as well as the Greek, was known to Bede, perhaps through the Greek Theodore of Tarsus. Like the women martyrs already mentioned, Anastasius was connected with Rome and was also commemorated in Bede's martyrology. The account when corrected provided an instance of heroic following of Christ, an example for Anglo-Saxons, to reinforce that of the first British martyr, Alban, which Bede had described in the *Ecclesiastical History*, rewriting the account he found in the *Life of St Germanus*.

The verse account of Felix, who was tortured for his faith in the third century, was written by his contemporary and admirer, Paulinus of Nola, and this formed the basis for Bede's *Life of St Felix*. Bede had a great respect for Paulinus and enjoyed his verses, but he was aware that few could do so. He therefore consistently simplified the text and made it into plain prose; it had to be available, understandable, in order to edify the new audience:

> The most blessed triumph of St Felix which, by the help of God he accomplished in Nola, a city in Campania, has been described by Paulinus, bishop of that city, most beautifully and fully in hexameter lines. But since prose is more suitable than verse for untrained readers, it has seemed right to me to make plain the story of this holy confessor in prose for the benefit of many.[19]

In his *Life of St Cuthbert* Bede had by him his own verse version as well as the account by an anonymous monk of Lindisfarne. It is the crown of Bede's work as a hagiographer-historian. Each chapter is an exploration in the light of the Bible of episodes in the life of the hermit-bishop who had lived so near to Bede in time and place. The subtle parallels of his verse version are put into clearer and fuller prose, while the slightly artificial biblical references with which the anonymous author surrounded his account of Cuthbert in Bede's hands became a powerful interpretation of the facts through one biblical text after another, with the understanding he had found of the Scriptures through the liturgy and the Fathers always in his mind. Bede said in his prefatory letter to Bishop Eadfrith that he had very carefully checked accounts given him of Cuthbert's life, that he had given references to the source of any new material he had included, and that the whole had been checked in detail by the community at Lindisfarne. But this care for accuracy of detail about the life of a man who had lived and died within living memory was only the basis for Bede's task; his main care was to link each event in the life of this Northumbrian monk with either the life and death of Christ or other biblical events, to bring out their significance and make them available to the reader. For instance, he begins with a reference to the Lamentations of Jeremiah that sets the theme for the whole work:

> The prophet Jeremiah consecrates for us the beginning of the life and miracles of the blessed father Cuthbert, when, praising the hermit's state of perfection, he says, 'It is good for a man to have borne the yoke in his youth; he sits alone and keeps silence because he has borne this upon him' (Lamentations 3:27–28).[20]

This verse was not arbitrarily chosen; it was the verse used in the readings at Night Office of Good Friday as the words of Christ in his passion, thus setting the theme of Bede's account of Cuthbert by relating it to the passion of Christ. When Bede recounted the story of the cure of Cuthbert's knee by a stranger before he became a monk, the stranger is described as 'an angel sent by one who once deigned to send the archangel Raphael to cure the eyes of Tobit'; it is significant that in his commentary on Tobit, Bede had consistently seen Raphael as a representation of Christ, healing Tobit, the devout Jew, that is, granting salvation to those who were already devout but not yet wholly given to Christ. Here, the 'healing' of Cuthbert is also a preface to his conversion from a good life to a more devout one: 'from this time the boy was wholly given to the Lord'.[21] Cuthbert was for Bede the ideal man of God, following God's will in 'the faith that works by love' whether as monk, prior, bishop or hermit; walking for weeks among the mountains to bring the Gospel to poor villagers; weeping with compassion before sinners even began their confessions; available to all, severe to none, but with his heart set upon the utter solitude of Farne, where he suffered alone and in great darkness, dying at the hour of prayer at night:

> He received ... the sacraments of salvation and fortified himself for his death which he knew had come now, by the communion of the Lord's Body and Blood, and raising his eyes to heaven and stretching out his hands aloft, he sent forth his spirit in the very act of praising God, to the joys of the heavenly Kingdom.[22]

SAINTS IN THE *ECCLESIASTICAL HISTORY*: LIFE, DEATH AND MIRACLES

These two works about Cuthbert were not Bede's only account of this saint. In Book Four of *The Ecclesiastical History of the English People* he gave a shorter version, this time as part of the plan of God for the conversion of England. Bede was always eager to praise former saints, whether those mentioned in the Bible or in the history of the Church; heaven was the fundamental dimension of all his writing; but the text in which he wrote most fully about saints of the immediate past was his last work, *The Ecclesiastical History of the English People*. It is a book full of accounts of saints which are 'true histories', combining both the care for facts of the historian with the insight of a theologian. Like Gregory the Great, Bede was ready to demonstrate to his readers that sanctity was not a far-away ideal of a distant past but something possible to people of his own land here and now. His information was copious and varied; he reworked what he had heard from those who knew about the recent past, as in the case of Hilda, Aidan, Oswald, Chad and Theodore, or from what he had read, as with the *Life of Fursa* and the accounts of Alban and Germanus. He also had information first-hand from his own acquaintance with such men as John of Hexham and Wilfrid of York. With certain of these accounts Bede was deeply involved, and the result is a series of classic saints' lives by a historian and theologian of unique ability and insight.

What Bede has to say about the saints was based upon carefully checked 'common report' but illuminated by reference to the Bible and also to commentaries on that text. It is no surprise that Bede's accounts of near-contemporary saints should be presented in images from the text with which he was so familiar. His method provided clues for his readers to whom the Bible was known with unimaginable detail and who would mine every phrase, every word, every syllable, of any biblical reference for significance, especially for what it had to say about the person of Christ and the soul of the reader. The biblical references in the *History* are integral to the text.

Virtues and miracles during life

There are three areas in lives of the saints described in the *Ecclesiastical History* which particularly illustrate this method of hagiography in which the Bible illuminates the account of a person. The first of these areas is that concerned with the two aspects of the saints during their lives: their virtues and their miracles. By what signs did men know that these people were living by a strength not their own? The words most often used about them by Bede are peace, love, joy, humility, kindness, mercy, and self-control. Of the virtues of Aidan he mentioned 'his love of peace and charity, temperance and humility';[23] with Hilda, he praised her both for teaching and for exemplifying the virtues of 'justice, devotion, chastity, but above all things . . . peace and charity'.[24] Both lists of virtues depend upon the Beatitudes (Matthew 5:3–12) and the fruits of the Spirit listed in Galatians 5:22, to which Bede frequently referred in his commentaries as the virtues of Christ and the apostles. In the *Ecclesiastical History* he connected Aidan's virtues with 'the commands of the evangelists, the apostles and the prophets', while with Hilda he suggested that the way of life she established at Whitby was 'after the example of the primitive church'. The 'virtues' of the Anglo-Saxon saints which Bede chose to praise were biblical in the smallest detail: for instance, he remarked several times that one of the virtues of Aidan and Chad was that instead of riding, they walked everywhere 'after the command of the Gospel'.[25] In his commentaries, Bede understood Luke 9:2, 10:9-11, and Acts 13:51 as commands to the apostles to go preaching on foot, and saw such behaviour, as indeed did the saints themselves, as signs that the apostolic preaching was still carried out. It was a mark of humility in a very literal sense, by which the preacher was close to *humus*, the earth. Such links between virtue and the Bible were of the first importance to Bede in presenting the saints because they were true signs of their likeness to Christ and also because they fulfilled the other obligation of the historian, to provide an example for others to imitate.

But the lives of the saints as Bede heard about them contained more than virtues; they were also filled with accounts of miracles. For Bede these were linked to the virtues and only had significance if they were seen as signs of God's action through those who lived in Christ: he wrote

> In vain is a miracle shown outwardly if there is lacking the inward disposition.[26]

Miracles were not just amazing but arbitrary events 'contrary to nature', but the signs of the blessing of God on the new Adam, of Christ the power of God at work in the bodies of living men. Aidan's miracles, for instance, demonstrated his Christ-like ability to control the four elements of fire, water, earth and air during his life. This could have indicated that Aidan was a magician, controlling and dominating creation, but for Bede, the way to sanctity was about the obedience of the four elements to the new Adam, Christ, and therefore those following him would have the same relationship to the whole of nature. Bede makes clear that it is the significance of such miracles that is important: 'He who judges the heart showed by signs and miracles what Aidan's virtues were'. Each of the saints in the *Ecclesiastical History* was shown to be blessed by God, but they are never presented as powerful wonder-workers. The 'miracles' Bede describes during the lifetimes of the saints were few in number, significant, and performed at the request of those in need. While men still lived, as Bede says in his commentaries, they would always be capable of sin, and any work of God performed through them could be an occasion for vainglory. Such miracles must therefore be attributed to the power of God able to act through their nature with the humble realization that this was limited by their own frailty. The care with which Pope Gregory had written to caution

Augustine of Canterbury on the subject of miracles was perhaps in his mind:

> Not all the elect work miracles, but nevertheless all their names are written in heaven. Therefore those who are true disciples ought not to rejoice except in the good thing they have in common with all the elect and which they will enjoy forever.[27]

Death and burial

Secondly, the most crucial point for Bede in a saint's life was his death. Just as the gospels are predominantly about the death and resurrection of Jesus, in quantity as well as in orientation, so the saints themselves approached death as the meeting place with the Saviour, the moment of their entry into life. From the first days of the Church the deaths of Christians had been described in terms deliberately recalling the death of Jesus. For example, when Stephen was stoned to death, the writer of Acts described his last words as direct quotations from those of Jesus on the Cross, 'Father forgive them' (Luke 23:34 and Acts 7:60) and 'Into thy hands I commend my spirit' (Luke 23:46 and Acts 7:61). The imagery of the cross and of the garden of the resurrection, white-robed figures, light, sweet smells, music, the images used at the end of each gospel to convey the opening of paradise through the resurrection of Christ, colour all other descriptions of Christian death. Bede's saints were no exception. Cuthbert saw the soul of Aidan carried up to heaven, 'amid the splendour of so great a light and accompanied by so many bands of angels'.[28] At the death of the abbess Eorcengota at dawn 'a crowd of men in white ... with a very great light and sweet fragrance' was seen coming 'to take back the gold coin which had been brought hither from Kent',[29] a reference to the gold piece of the parable that was lost and found combined with the fact that the princess had originally come from Kent. The nun Begu saw a great light when her abbess Hilda was dying:

> A light poured in from above filled the whole place ... she saw the soul of the handmaiden of the Lord being borne to heaven in the midst of that light, attended and guided by angels.[30]

At the death of Chad, sweet singing was heard in the sky with a great light.[31] The message was in each case the same: for at least some people in Anglo-Saxon England, death had proved the gateway to life everlasting.

Posthumous miracles

Thirdly, where death was a beginning for the saints and not an end, such everlasting life was not divorced from life in time. Bede saw the work of God continuing in England in his day through the prayers of the saints. One of the attractions of Christianity for the Anglo-Saxons was its perspective of a wider reality which lay around their lives:

> If this new doctrine brings more certain information about what follows or indeed what went before [the life of a man on earth] it seems right that we should accept it.[32]

Bede was always conscious of the Anglo-Saxons as a small part of the whole Church of God, most of which was already in heaven, and his accounts of saints of the past were linked to the present, where God still acted through his elect now and in England. Bede's historical sense reached into the past of the early Church with enthusiasm but not only with antiquarian zeal; the saints were success stories and they were alive in God, available to prayer. The lives of Anglo-Saxons who were known as saints illustrated most of all to Bede, and through him to his contemporaries, that life here and now was open towards this other dimension, that life on earth was still the threshold of the kingdom of God. In the *Ecclesiastical History* saints are seen in this perspective: some of them like Fursa and Drythelm, an Irish hermit and a married Saxon householder, had visionary experiences of the next world while they were still alive and Bede recorded their accounts very fully for the warning of his readers. The gate between the worlds was not entirely closed when the saints had passed through in death. Children heard themselves called, messages came back, saints came to lead each other home. Heaven, and therefore the possibility of hell, was the true dimension of human life, here and now.

One material fact in particular about death interested Bede. The actual state of the physical remains of the saints was to him a sign of the resurrection and a pledge of the Kingdom. In the case of certain saints, their flesh remained whole and incorrupt after death, and when Bede recorded such accounts he was very careful not to leave such things as mere wonders, though how they were to be interpreted was not always clear. In the case of Queen Aethelthryth, Bede saw her incorruption as a sign of her virginity of body and in this he suggested she followed the example of Christ himself. But at the abbey of Brie, near Meaux, the body that was found to be incorrupt was not that of the marvellous English nun and virgin

Eorcengota, from whose tomb arose sweet scents, but her aunt, Aethelburgh, an abbess of Brie of rather more worldly concerns. She had been so busy building for herself a magnificent church around her tomb that it was unfinished when she died and remained so. Bede notes that her body was found to be incorrupt after seven years and that this was a surprise to everyone; he concluded that this had happened because God knew more clearly than men that she 'had remained immune from fleshly desires'.[33]

A less ambiguous instance was the fact that the body of Cuthbert of Lindisfarne was found to be incorrupt eleven years after death. Bede described it in the fourth book of his *Ecclesiastical History*:

> Opening the grave they found the body intact and whole as if it were still alive, the joints of the limbs flexible and much more like a sleeping man than a dead one.[34]

In line with Bede's view of the present age as running concurrently with the seventh age in which the saints rested before the general resurrection, Cuthbert was described as 'asleep' and 'alive', this life extending even in his flesh. Fursa the Irish preacher, visionary and hermit, had also been found incorrupt four years after his death in Lagny; Bede knew this by reading an account of Fursa and he says he included the account of incorruption from this in his version 'so that readers might clearly know how eminent a man he was'. His 'eminence' was for Bede connected with his visionary experiences, which had already in life marked his flesh: Bede had been told by a monk of Jarrow that someone who had met Fursa in East Anglia noted that during the hardest weather he wore only a thin garment

> and sweated as though it were the middle of the summer because of either the terror or the joy of his recollections.[35]

But the sign of incorruption remained a mysterious matter; often Bede connects it with virginity of body, but not always. It could happen to a secular king as well as to a hermit; the arm of Oswald was kept incorrupt at Bamburgh in Bede's day, a matter he connected with Oswald's almsgiving and his blessing by Aidan.

Another instance of this theological approach to the accounts of the saints is in the details Bede selects when describing the places where they were buried. The location for the burial or reburial of the saints is described by Bede as 'on the right side of the altar'. It is no doubt a factual description but it was far more significant than that, both for the Christians of Anglo-Saxon England and for their historian. In his didactic works, Bede had seen the right hand as the hand signifying what is good and in his commentaries the right side always carried this positive significance. In the description of the Temple in the Old Testament the phrase 'on the right side' in 'The door for the middle chamber was in the right side of the house; and they went up with winding stairs into the the middle chamber and out of the middle into the third' (1 Kings 6:8) suggested to Bede the piercing of the right side of Christ on the Cross by a spear. He saw the 'right side' therefore as the way of entry of the saints into heaven, which is the heart of Christ:

> Certainly this place is rightly seen to be the body of the Lord which he took from the Virgin . . . When the Lord was dead on the Cross 'one of the soldiers opened his side with a lance' (John 19:34). It is well said 'in the right side of the house' because holy church believes that it was his right side that was opened by the soldier. Here aptly does the evangelist use this word, so as not to say the side was 'pierced' or 'wounded' but 'opened', that is to say as if a door in the midst of the side had been set open by which the way to heaven has been set open for us. Then is added, 'and at once there came out blood and water': that is, water by which we are washed in baptism and blood which we consecrate in the holy chalice. For by this there is a door for us to ascend in the midst of the second and from the midst of the third, because we ascend by faith and the mystery of our redemption from the present conversation of the church to the rest of souls after death, and again from the rest of souls at the coming of the day of Judgement to immortality of our bodies also, as if in the third we will penetrate to a more sublime stage yet . . . where we will live in perpetual beatitude of soul and body.[36]

It was with this hope in mind that Bede noted the place of Cuthbert's burial at Lindisfarne:

> It was buried in a stone coffin on the right-hand side of the altar in the church of the blessed apostle Peter.[37]

Equally theological was Bede's understanding of miracles connected with the bones of the saints at their tombs. There the poor and sick were healed, but the importance of this to Bede lay not so much in the wonder of cures or the health of the people concerned as in the fact that those who were dead had 'entered in through the right side' and so were nearer to Christ. There they were not more distant from their fellow-Christians but nearer and more able to help them. They were, as a sign of the last age, more available to prayer. Bede recommended prayer *for* the dead:

> Beseech the souls who have preceded it to heaven to aid its beginnings by their good example and by recalling to it the beginning, course and enduring of the road of virtue which they travelled.[38]

but prayer also *to* the dead:

> Through the intercession of the saints who shine, not through their own power but from him, Christ will be propitious to the faithful when they raise their minds to heavenly desires and recognise his glory in the words and deeds of the preceding fight.[39]

Bede's commentaries on the Bible are full of this perspective of life as a pilgrimage towards the real homeland, a continuous putting on of the Lord Jesus here but with the real fullness of manhood only begun to be realized after death. The saints in heaven did not abandon those still on earth. Those closer to Christ shared more in his power of love, not less, and in Bede's accounts of the death and burial of the saints, miracles abounded of love and grace and healing.

CONTEMPORARY SAINTS

Not all Bede's saints had died before he was born. In his *History of the Abbots of Wearmouth–Jarrow* Bede wrote from first-hand knowledge and in the *Ecclesiastical History* he had known at least Wilfrid and John of Hexham, some of whose miracles he recorded and whom he venerated as saints. Like Gregory the Great in the *Dialogues*, Bede wrote about modern instances of sanctity among people whom he himself had known, for the encouragement of his contemporaries. Of his abbots he had no miracles to record; perhaps this had no part in an account of a monastic house, with the greater miracles of love and peace and humility in daily life. It was with bishops, involved in preaching and teaching, that Bede does not hesitate to associate wonders in connection with their ministry. In his experience as a monk at Jarrow what was significant was, for instance, the humility of Eosterwine, who died aged 36 as the second abbot of Jarrow. He had been a thane of King Ecgfrith and was related to Benedict Biscop; 'of cheerful disposition, liberally generous and distinguished looking', he nevertheless always shared in the manual work of the brothers. With them, he undertook

> the winnowing and threshing, the milking of the ewes and cows; he laboured in bakehouse, garden and kitchen, taking part cheerfully and obediently in every monastery chore.[40]

It was charity and humility that Bede recorded as the sign of the presence of God among his brothers and this was so even when he wrote about Ceolfrith, whom he had known and loved with a special admiration:

> [He was] a man of acute mind, conscientious in everything he did, of mature judgement, fervent and zealous for his faith.[41]

It was not about these men that Bede recorded external wonders but in connection with bishops such as Aidan, Cuthbert, Wilfrid and John of Beverley; it was through them in support of their ministry of preaching that God manifested miracles.

The saints were remembered each year liturgically on the anniversary of their deaths. The calendar of the saints set them in the perspective of the whole Church, and their yearly commemoration continued to give them a place within time. Bede put together a calendar which combined two of his interests, sanctity and time. The saints were people with their own personal histories but these were given a new significance in eternity where they remained available in time each year especially through the liturgy. Bede's calendar, immediately adopted and added to, as one of the major martyrologies of the Church,[42] contained the commemoration not only of biblical persons, such as the apostles and the Virgin Mary, and those of the early Church such as the martyrs, but also the Anglo-Saxon dead like Cuthbert and Benedict Biscop. Like the saints of the remote past, the saints of Wearmouth and Jarrow were 'alive unto God' and therefore remembered in the church of Jarrow each year in the liturgy as friends who now lived more closely with the Lord.

It is in this liturgical perspective that Bede wrote about the saints, but this did not cause him to produce stilted or formal accounts of them. On the contrary, his awareness of the immediate availability of the saints, to help, encourage and edify made his accounts of them especially lively. For him they were still vividly alive and it is this quality which makes Bede's account of the saints of England especially readable and immediate. Very many of the early English and Irish saints who are still so attractive more than a thousand years later are known only from the pages of Bede. Bede is the only source for information about Hilda, northern princess and abbess of Whitby, who died when Bede was a young monk; the gentle and uncomplaining Chad, with his devout brothers Cedd, Cynebill and Caelin; Aidan, the apostle of Northumbria, and friend of Oswald and Oswine; the Merovingian wife of Aethelberht, Bertha of Kent, and their daughter Aethelburgh. Equally memorable are his pictures of the plain Christians of England: Caedmon the cowherd poet; Drythelm the father of a family in Cunningham, who after visionary experience of hell retired to Melrose and in winter would stand in the river Tweed with broken pieces of ice floating around him and when asked how he could bear it replied simply 'I have known it colder'; the Irish visionary Fursa who built a monastery in East Anglia with his brothers Foillan and Ultan, lived in solitude and then visited Clovis of the Franks in Gaul where he ended his life in peace. The *Ecclesiastical History* is a moving account of the initial work of the Word of God among English men and women in places and in ways entirely familiar:

> The humble of heart will hear the Word of God and do it and they will refer all the good they do, not to their own praise, but to the praise and glory of their heavenly benefactor. And so, rightly being fed with the bread of life they will attain to that eternal life which is of the inward man.[43]

Notes

1 *Revelation* 2:28, col. 140.

2 *Epistles: 1 Peter* 1:12, p. 76.

3 *Genesis* 4:17, p. 86.

4 *Habakkuk* 3:19, p. 408.

5 *Mark* 9:5–6, p. 544.

6 *Homilies* I, 4, p. 26.

7 *Luke* 1:46, p. 37.

8 *Homilies* I, 4, p. 24.

9 Ibid., p. 30.

10 *Homilies* I, 7, p. 48.

11 HA (Farmer), 6, p. 190.

12 *Homilies* II, 20, p. 144.

13 *Homilies* I, 21, p. 149.

14 HE, IV.20, pp. 397–401.

15 *Temple*, p. 163.

16 Cf. Patrick Wormald, 'Bede and Benedict Biscop' in *Famulus Christi*, pp. 141–70.

17 Paul the Deacon, Homily III, *De Sancto Patre Benedicto* (PL 95, 1574). Cf. G. Morin, *Revue Bénédictine* XI (1892), pp. 316–26.

18 HE, V.24, pp. 571–3. See *Bibliotheca hagiographica latina* (2 vols, Brussels, 1898–1901), nos 408–13 for versions of this *Life*. For a most illuminating discussion of the three texts, cf. C. Vircillo Franklin and P. Meyvaert, *Analecta Bollandiana* 100 (1982), pp. 373–400.

19 *Felix*, Preface, col. 784. Cf. Thomas W. Mackay, 'Bede's hagiographical method: his knowledge and use of Paulinus of Nola' in *Famulus Christi*, pp. 77–92.

20 VSC, 1, p. 155. For the use of Tenebrae readings at Jarrow see my article 'The spirituality of St Cuthbert' in *St Cuthbert, his Cult and his Community*, ed. G. Bonner, D. W. Rollason and C. Stancliffe (London, 1989), pp. 65–77.

21 VSC, 3, p. 161.

22 VSC, 39, p. 285.

23 For Bede's account of Aidan, see HE, III.5, pp. 227–9; III.17, p. 267.

24 For Bede's account of Hilda, see HE, IV.23, pp. 404–14.

25 HE, III.5, p. 227; IV.3, p. 337.

26 *Mark* 3:14, p. 470 (quoting Gregory the Great). For discussion of Bede's attitude to miracles see Bertram Colgrave, 'Bede's miracle stories' in BLTW, pp. 201–30; Benedicta Ward, 'Miracles and history: a reconsideration of the miracle stories used by Bede' in *Famulus Christi*, pp. 70–7.

27 HE, I.31, p. 109.

28 VSC, 4, p. 167.

29 HE, III.8, p. 239.

30 Ibid., IV.23, p. 413.

31 Ibid., IV.3, p. 341.

32 Ibid., II.13, p. 185.

33 Ibid., III.8, p. 241.

34 Ibid., IV.30, pp. 443–5.

35 Ibid., III.9, p. 275. Incorruption of a body after death could equally well indicate extreme wickedness, since the earth refused to accept the body after death.

36 *Temple*, 1 Kings 6:8, pp. 165-6; *Song of Songs* 11:5, p. 215.

37 VSC, 40, p. 289.

38 *Song of Songs* 11:5, p. 215.

39 *Genesis* 9:13-15, p. 135.

40 HA (Farmer), 8, p. 193.

41 Ibid., 15, p. 200.

42 See *Edition pratique des martyrologes de Bède, de l'Anonyme lyonnais et de Florus*, ed. J. Dubois and G. Renaud (Institut de Recherche et d'Histoire des Textes, Paris, 1976).

43 *Luke* 11:28, p. 237.

5

Bede and the English

The end of the *Ecclesiastical History of the English People*, the greatest work of history produced in the barbarian world, presents a picture of unity and peace, a climax of paradise restored:

> In these favourable times of peace and prosperity, many of the Northumbrian race, both noble and simple, have laid aside their weapons and taken the tonsure. . . . This is the state of the whole of Britain at the present time, about 285 years after the coming of the English to Britain, in the year of our Lord 731.[1]

This state of peace and unity was, of course, not factually true, and Bede knew it to be so. He expressed his reservations about his own times very forcibly a little later in his letter to Bishop Egbert, in particular forcing home his condemnation of the weaknesses within the widespread monastic life which in the *History* he had praised. What Bede was describing at the end of the *Ecclesiastical History*, after this story of setbacks, failures, and steady progress, was a vision, a promise and a hope. All that he had described as good in the past could issue in a society as without rank as the early Church, where weapons would be beaten into ploughshares, and the kingdom of God surely established in England's green and pleasant land. Peace and unity, the two virtues most stressed in all Bede's writings, could prevail, and had in fact already found some visible expression in spite of the fact that whatever he had described as working for evil and division also had its effects. He added to his conclusion two quotations from Psalm 96(97):1, 'the multitude of the isles may be glad' and Psalm 29(30):5(4), 'give thanks unto him for a remembrance of his holiness', psalms interpreted by the Fathers with reference to the resurrection and salvation:

> The earth restored is the resurrection of the flesh . . . the word of God has been preached not to the continent alone but also in those isles which lie in the midst of the sea; even these are full of Christians, full of the word of God.[2]
>
> He has not forgotten the sanctification wherewith he has sanctified you.[3]

When Bede applied these verses to the island of Britain he was writing theology rather than history. What he meant by 'peace' was not an earthly agreement to cease hostilities, but peace between God and man. In a sermon for Easter he explained clearly what the peace was that he cherished:

> The whole mission of our Redeemer in the flesh was to restore peace to the world. It was for this that he became man, for this he suffered, for this he rose from the dead: that by appeasing him, he might bring us back to the peace of God, who by offending God have incurred his anger.[4]

The fact that the *Ecclesiastical History* ends with such a vision of hope is a warning that this is not a modern history, describing the activities of the Anglo-Saxons, with peculiar omissions. It is *ecclesiastica*, theology, applied to *historia*, common account; in other words, through its presentation of what was generally agreed about accounts of past events, it reveals the pattern of redemption, the work of God in this world and the next. The impression that this book is a work of modern critical history is misleading. It is partly derived from the Preface, where Bede described, with careful detail, the sources, written and oral, upon which he relied. Throughout the book this constant care about factual evidence and sources suggests at once a Stubbs or a Toynbee at work. But sources are not all; the modern historian also tries to see that the information he has gathered is presented with objectivity and completeness. It is here that Bede belongs to an older world of historical writing and he says so in the same Preface:

> Should history tell of good men and their good estate, the thoughtful reader is spurred on to imitate the good; should it record the evil deeds of wicked men, no less effectually the devout and earnest listener or reader is kindled to eschew what

is harmful and perverse and himself with greater care pursue those things which he has learned to be good and pleasing in the sight of God.[5]

For Bede, as for Thucydides and Herodotus, history was a part of rhetoric, and it was more specifically, as for Eusebius, a part of Christian rhetoric, or teaching. He was not writing only a record of past events but selecting and presenting those past events for the use of the present and the future. It was the good of the readers and hearers he had in mind, not only loyalty to the dead.

This view of the purpose of history had its effect on the ensuing text and in the same Preface, when Bede says that he has written his book 'in accordance with the principles of true history' (*quod vera lex historiae est*) these principles turn out to be very different from a plain assembly of facts. He explains that such 'principles' mean that he has 'sought to commit to writing what I have collected from common report for the instruction of posterity', an understanding of 'true history' not common today.[6] 'True history' is a phrase used by Bede elsewhere; in his commentary on the gospel of Luke he says that when Luke mentions Joseph in his account of the presentation of Christ in the Temple and refers to Joseph as 'the father of Jesus' this was not in contradiction to the fact that he had previously described Jesus as conceived by the Holy Ghost and born of a virgin.[7] It is rather that here Luke was recording the *popular opinion* that Joseph was the father of Jesus. It is this 'popular opinion' that Bede describes as *quae vera historiae lex est*, a phrase he may well have found in Jerome's comment on the same passage, 'as the Evangelist said, giving popular opinion, *quae vera historiae lex est*'.[8] Neither Jerome nor Bede thought for one moment that it was *true* that Joseph was the father of Jesus; to them, he was the Son of God born of a virgin. What they meant by the 'true law of history' was a careful record of popular report. If it was to become useful for the instruction and edification of the readers, something more needed to be done with popular report in the way of interpreting it according to known truth revealed in Christ. In the case of Luke's phrase they are saying that this popular report was wrong; that theological insight is a surer guide to truth than what is thought by everybody and that it may in fact contradict that opinion.

This view of 'true history' was fundamental to Bede's historical work. It was with this in mind that he received accounts from many sources, written and oral; these came to him as *verax historicus*, that is, 'that which was indeed told'; he checked most earnestly to be sure what it was that was being said, and then rewrote this agreed report to bring out the greater truth of redemption which transcended the 'true law of history'. In the *Ecclesiastical History* Bede presented many such received opinions about the past but he consistently reworked such accounts in order to present their inner truth in accordance with the insights of theology. To illustrate this further, Bede used the same phrase in connection with the life of Aidan, where he says he had written *quasi verax historicus*, reporting Aidan's views on Easter, which were well-known, not to agree with them, but as part of the common report of his life, while showing also his undoubted evangelical goodness. What Bede had to say, therefore, in his *History* was based upon 'common report' but illuminated by reference to Christian revelation above all as found in the primary source for all his works, the Bible.

THE STRUCTURE OF THE *ECCLESIASTICAL HISTORY*

The whole of the *Ecclesiastical History* has a strong framework, intricately worked with overlapping detail, and it is as much a theology as a history. This becomes clear when it is seen as the climax of Bede's works, as the last of the commentaries, only in this case it is commentary on a new people of God rather than on the record of the people of the two covenants. Moreover Bede's *Ecclesiastical History* had its place within his structure for world history, which he so often described. He saw the whole of history as divided into six 'ages', corresponding to the six days in which God created the world, and also to the six ages of man who is the microcosm of creation, which was Bede's own addition to this tradition. Five of these 'ages' were past, the sixth still in progress. While in one sense, the whole history of the Anglo-Saxons was part of the sixth age, yet when looking back from his own position in the sixth age, Bede structured his account of their past in the form of five 'ages', leading up to the present sixth age of Christ.[9] There were five books about the past in the *Ecclesiastical History* which was being written in the sixth age, a number which may have attracted Bede also by its correspondence with the five books of the Pentateuch, the history of the people of the Old Covenant.[10]

In *De Temporum Ratione*, Bede explained his theory of the ages of the world. The first age began after the fall of Adam, which was the beginning of temporal history:

> Now the first age of this world is from Adam up to Noah . . .
> the first age [infancy] of every man.

The first book of the *Ecclesiastical History* is about the infancy of Christianity among the Anglo-Saxons. Augustine was sent to 'preach the Word of life' and to 'baptize' the English, in other words to bring them to birth. The second age, from Noah to Abraham, was 'the childhood of the race of the people of God . . . in which language was invented': the second book deals with the growth of the English Church and the passing of the first generation of converts, ending with an account of how James the Deacon brought music, the full articulation of words, to York in the conversion of the north. The third age, from Noah up to David, was 'the youth of the people of God . . . when a man begins to propagate his kind', and corresponds to the fruitful life of the Church in Northumbria described in the third book, while the fourth age, 'from David to the emigration to Babylon', when 'the time of kings began among the people of God as it were from this mature age', is linked to the fourth book and the establishment of firm leadership for the Church under its 'princes', Theodore and Hadrian. The fifth age was 'as it were old age, from the migration to Babylon until the coming of the Saviour' when 'the Hebrew people were shattered by frequent misfortune as though weary with the weight of age'. In Book Five, for the year 729 Bede recorded that 'two comets appeared' which seemed 'to portend dire disaster to east and west alike' and 'to indicate that mankind was threatened by calamities by day and by night'. This sense of the end of things was continued and emphasized in Bede's letter to Egbert of York about 'the sad state in which our nation miserably labours'. The present meant a running-down of the world through the sixth age now in progress, of which 'no course of generations or times is certain' except that 'as being the age of senility, it is to be consummated by the death of all the world'. This sixth age, however, ran concurrently with the seventh age in which

> Those who by a happy death conquered those toilsome ages of the world, full of labours, are now taken into the seventh age of the eternal sabbath and await the eighth age of the Resurrection in which they shall reign forever with the Lord.

Each of the five books of the *Ecclesiastical History* is filled with the vision of those saints already at rest in the seventh age, though still available to the toilers in the sixth. Bede's account of the English is therefore a world history in miniature, in which they take their place among the people of God awaiting the 'eighth age of the blessed Resurrection in which they shall reign forever with the Lord'.

In writing his account of the ecclesiastical history of his own race in the sixth age of the world, Bede wrote within a well-established tradition of Church history. He had read the early Church historians and among them it was Eusebius whom he saw most clearly as his predecessor. Like Eusebius, Bede transcribed into his *History* official documents, letters, acts of Councils, and like him he saw such texts as a vital basis for an account of the life of the Church. Like Eusebius also, he regarded the history of the people of God as it had been written in the Old Testament as a record of a covenant relationship and saw the gospels and Acts as a continuation of this with its account of the people of the New Covenant. But unlike Eusebius, Bede did not summarize this salvation history in order to show its continuity with that of the early Church, and his concern was with one nation only. It was 'a history of the Church of our island and race', an account of a single nation, the English, a new generation of the people of God, being prepared, by reading this work itself as well as by other means, for the last 'age' of heaven, the kingdom of God.

BOOK ONE

The 'ages of the world' and the biblical concept of salvation history were not the only structures for the *Ecclesiastical History*. The scheme was also held together by themes which are woven into each book and here the long training of Bede in biblical commentary is evident. Book One begins with a prelude, a background, and in it the main themes of the book are also presented. First, as in the commentaries, Bede was concerned to ascertain as far as he could from previous writers the physical external facts, in this case the actual geographical situation of the island of Britain. With precise detail he established the island in relation to temporal space:

> Britain, once called Albion, is an island of the ocean ... it extends 800 miles to the north and is 200 miles broad ... the whole circuit of the coastline covers 3,875 miles, its space 800 by 200, and 8 by 20.[11]

But these facts were not there for their own sake; these first sentences dealt with the formation of sea and land, as in the first book of the Bible, and Bede next described the riches of the island, still following the sequence set out in Genesis for God's creation of the world: fruits of the earth, and trees; cattle, fowls of the air,

116

fishes of the sea and the minerals in the earth. The races and the languages of those who inhabited this paradise were then described. The parallel with Genesis was intended to indicate the primal innocence of this new creation, as well as to situate it geographically.

The following chapters describe the place of the island in time as well as space. Bede always saw England in relation to the rest of the world, and he therefore referred to Roman emperors and used the imperial dating system. But the place of the island in the early Christian world predominated. Dates regulated by the birth of Christ linked Britain with the Incarnation, and two aspects of the history of the early Church he showed to have had their counterpart in Britain. The British had participated in the martyrdoms of the early days through the death of Alban, and Britain had its place in the early heresies by producing the monk Pelagius and therefore Pelagianism. Moreover, Britain had a share in the early preaching of the Gospel by the mission from Gaul of Bishop Germanus of Auxerre (*c.* 378–448)

A more tragic parallel was presented here also. As in Genesis, so also early British history, as Bede read about it in Gildas's *The Ruin of Britain*, contained the story of a Fall, of a Christianity established but lost by sin. This exile of the British Christians from the life of the universal Church was a matter of continual and deep concern for Bede. Those who went out from this Eden, the British, he saw as perversely remaining outside redemption until their partial return is described in the last chapters of the whole work. Chapter 24 of Book One ends with this failure of the British Christians but also a promise of their reconciliation: 'his goodness did not reject the people whom he knew'.

From this account of Britain Bede passed smoothly to the main theme of his work, the conversion of the Anglo-Saxons. The British, Bede says, did not concern themselves with the conversion of their conquerors and he described the missionaries sent by Gregory the Great to Anglo-Saxon England as 'much worthier heralds of the truth'. The next ten chapters contain Bede's account of the mission of Augustine and his reception by Aethelberht of Kent, the birth of that king into new life by baptism, and the establishment of a burial place for the bishops and kings as they entered fully into the rest of heaven. Bede's interest in both the Fathers of the Church and the matter of preaching to the English caused him to devote a large amount of space to the letters of Augustine and Pope Gregory about the Kentish mission.

The penultimate chapter of Book One seems at first to be the natural climax of the book, with Christianity visibly established with the founding by king and bishop together of the church which later became Canterbury Cathedral and the abbey later known as St Augustine's. But the chapter which ends the first book in fact contains a more solemn note of warning. Christianity was beginning to flourish in Kent and the bodies of the saints were already buried in English soil to await the resurrection in the last age, but elsewhere the way back to paradise was not restored. It is at this point that Aethelfrith, the pagan king of Northumbria, Bede's own province, is introduced into the narrative by a reference to the battle of Degsastan, in which he won a definitive victory over the Irish 'at the same time' as the events in Kent. The mention of Aethelfrith in this book is not accidental. In a literary sense, it gives notice that the unconverted north is to be the centre of interest later, and it is with his name in Book Three that Bede introduces Aethelfrith's son Oswald, destined to be the most Christian king of Northumbria. Secondly, Aethelfrith is described here as the scourge of God to chastise the British and the Irish, those rejectors of God whose reconciliation, either by conviction or by defeat, became a constant theme of the whole work. The pagan ruler is compared to Saul in the Old Testament, used by God, though in the end rejected. There are other examples later in the *Ecclesiastical History* of rulers, such as Penda of Mercia, who were not themselves Christian, yet who were used by God as the instrument of the chastisement of an unfaithful people. By introducing Aethelfrith the pagan at this point in the text, and describing him as 'Saul', the first but rejected king of Israel, Bede introduced a theme, still in parallel with the Bible, of kingship, indicating that its connection with Christianity was not a straightforward matter of celestial patronage. The last sentence of Book One reaffirms the wider context of the work by linking the date of the battle of Degsastan with the year 603 from the Incarnation and also the first year of the reign of the emperor Phocas.[12]

BOOK TWO

Book Two continues the story of the newly-born people of God from Book One, beginning with the year 605 and the death of Gregory the Great, the hero of the mission just described. For Bede, Gregory was 'our apostle' and the eulogy he wrote shows his admiration for the saint as the mastermind behind the mission, and also shows comprehensive and thorough knowledge of his works, a fact amply borne out in the *Commentaries*. At its conclusion he added as 'a tradition received from our ancestors' the well-known story of Gregory and the English slave-boys, a significant instance of Bede's preference for the significant over the factual. The whole chapter presents Gregory, a patron saint by whose prayers all the future of the English Church will be protected.[13] The rest of Book Two continues the story of the conversion in the south, with setbacks and failures as well as progress. The British, in England, Wales and Ireland, occupy first place, with the account of Augustine's vain attempts to exercise his apostolic authority over the British Church: a story presumably from a Welsh rather than a Kentish source, since it does not show Augustine in an amiable light. Bede's condemnation of heretics was always severe and he concludes his description of their rejection of Augustine by quoting a warning the bishop gave them:

> If they refused to accept peace from their brethren, they would have to accept war from their enemies; and if they would not preach the way of life to the English nation, they would one day suffer the vengeance of death at their hands.[14]

Once more, it was the pagan northerner, Aethelfrith, who wreaked vengeance on the heretics. Again, Bede saw him as the unwitting sword of the Lord against not the Irish this time but the Welsh, to the advantage of Augustine and the English. The severity of Bede's point of view is emphasized by his account of the slaughter of the British Christian monks from Bangor who had prayed for Aethelfrith and his men on the field of battle. In this Bede's opinion that those who pray should be protected was subordinated to his belief that their destruction was a doom caused by their apostasy.

The mission expanded; Mellitus and Justus were consecrated as bishops and Mellitus began his episcopate in London among the East Angles, while Justus was placed in the new see of Rochester, a sure indication that the description of the increase in numbers of Christians by baptism had not been exaggerated. In this 'second age' of the childhood of the English Church, both Aethelberht and Augustine died. With their successors, the fragile nature of the Church was demonstrated. Augustine was succeeded by another of the first monk-missionaries, Laurence, and while Aethelberht lived all went well. Laurence's first act as archbishop was concerned with unity, and he urged both the Irish and the British into closer union with the English–Roman Church, but in vain. The death of

Aethelberht of Kent, however, demonstrated the dependence of the Christian bishops upon the king and their impotence under successors neither Christian nor friendly. Eadbald, son of Aethelberht by a pagan wife, had not been baptized, unlike the daughter of Aethelberht by Queen Bertha. He followed pagan Germanic customs, such as marrying his father's widow, causing scandal to the Christians at court, to such an extent that the archbishop prepared to leave and return to Gaul. Among the East Saxons, too, on the death of Saeberht his pagan heirs molested the Christians so that they fled. Bede's account of the resolution of the problem for the Church was not about a superficial matter of discussion and treaty. Laurence, preparing to leave England next day, slept in the church at St Peter and St Paul, and prayed with tears for his Church:

> As he slept, the blessed prince of the apostles appeared to him, and in the dead of night scourged him hard and long.[15]

The example of Peter, who had suffered death rather than abandon his mission, was thus driven home. In this account Bede drew a significant contrast for his readers between Christianity and paganism. A basic theme for pagan religion was that if affairs did not turn out well, either the sacrifices had been mistakenly offered, but more usually the gods had failed; and given the choice provided by polytheism, it was time to move on to other gods. This view of disaster as defeat rather than opportunity had infected Laurence but the scourging reminded him of the central fact of his faith, that when disaster strikes a Christian he has nowhere else to go; God is God, however uncomfortable the believer, and so another explanation must be found to cope with this. Laurence found it in suffering, a reminder of the central fact of the Cross for Christianity, and he convinced Eadbald to the point of baptism.

The next chapters of Book Two were connected with the theme which was fully developed in Book Three, that is, the conversion of Northumbria, Bede's own land. However, these chapters also provided a link with the Kentish mission of Book One by describing Paulinus and the Roman missionaries sent north with Aethelburgh, the daughter of Aethelberht and Bertha, upon her marriage to the pagan Edwin of Northumbria. The conversion of Edwin and descriptions of his reign provide a complex picture of the way in which war, alliance, marriage and baptism all played their part in conversion. The decision of Edwin to be baptized was not only a matter of conviction. As with Aethelberht in Kent, the influence of a Christian wife and her chaplain played a part; so, too, did political alliance, defeat and exile, as well as visions, dreams and serious thought about Christianity on Edwin's part. For this king as for Aethelberht, the decision to become a Christian was not taken in isolation:

> He said he would confer about this with his loyal chief men and his counsellors, so that if they agreed with him, they might all be consecrated together in the waters of baptism.[16]

By contrast, the instance of a failure of a king to establish Christianity in his kingdom described in this book is that of Raedwald of East Anglia, who was baptized alone, far from home and without consultation of his wife or advisers.

Papal letters of affection and guidance, the building of churches, baptisms, and a peace so great

> that a woman with a newborn child could walk throughout the island from sea to sea and take no harm[17]

fill the last pages of this section of the history; but, like Book One, it does not end on this note of satisfaction. Bede deliberately included a more solemn chapter at the end, again describing military defeat at the hands of another pagan ruler, this time Penda of Mercia, in the battle of Hatfield Close in 633. This time, those defeated were Christian and in recording this fact, Bede is able to make another theological point: conversion and the blessing of God were no guarantee of worldly success; the Christian kings were not in the pattern of the Old Testament rulers in that respect at least.

BOOK THREE

Book Three begins with a chapter of disaster under three kings so extreme that Bede says that year was not counted among the years of man on earth. Osric, a nephew of Edwin, had been among those baptized by Paulinus, and Eanfrith, Aethelfrith's son, had received baptism while in exile among the Irish. But on claiming the thrones of Deira and Bernicia, they

> abjured and betrayed the mysteries of the heavenly kingdom to which they had been admitted and reverted to the filth of their former idolatry.[18]

Apostasy and heresy for Bede were always more culpable than paganism and the defeat of these two is presented by him as a judgement of God. Although it was a Christian king who was used by God for this vengeance, Caedwalla of Gwynedd was a Welsh prince, and therefore, to Bede's mind, outside the unity of the Church; he destroyed the two apostates who were in an even more lamentable state. The fall of the British Caedwalla and his 'outrageous tyranny' followed, however, and this time the sword of the Lord was wielded by a Christian, the royal saint-hero of the book, Oswald of Northumbria.

Oswald is presented by Bede at the crucial battle of Denisesburn as one who, like the Emperor Constantine, fought against great odds under the sign of the cross, and was given the victory through prayer and dependence on God in a just cause. In this central book, Bede recounted the glories of the reigns of the most Christian kings Oswald, Oswine and Oswiu, along with the beauty of the Irish mission in the hands of Aidan, Columba and Colman, as the third age of the English Church, the age of youth, a new stage in the articulation of the faith. Absorbed as he was by giving an account of his own part of England, as in the previous books, Bede did not forget the wider world, and descriptions of visits by kings and nobles as well as clergy to Rome and Gaul were mentioned as being even more frequent. This is not either a nationalist or a self-congratulatory account. In spite of the dominating figure of Oswald as the saint-king of the north, blessed by God and displaying apostolic virtues, the picture of these years that Bede presented was by no means a simple demonstration of providence at work in politics, approving the converted by success. Oswine, the successor of Oswald in Bernicia, Bede described as a good king and a good Christian, a close friend of Aidan, an attractive man and one who inspired loyalty and affection in his subjects. But he was murdered by his Christian co-ruler Oswiu, the hero of the next part of the book. Bede's praise of the kings was by no means without censure; like both Saul and David, they made mistakes, but these could be redeemed by repentance, in this case by the building of the monastery at Gilling, over which his widow Eanflaed, the daughter of Edwin, later presided as abbess.

The mission to Northumbria presented Bede with a chance to praise the monks and clergy in Northumbria, as heirs of the apostles, as true missionaries. Aidan, he says,

> made it his business to omit none of the commands of the apostles, the evangelists and the prophets, but he set himself to carry them out in his deeds as far as he was able.[19]

The seeds of English monastic life had already been sown in Kent; in this book, Bede mentioned and praised English women who became nuns at the abbey of Brie in Gaul and the royal English monastery at Bardney, but even more eagerly he wrote about the Irish monks, Columba of Iona, Fursa and Colman from Ireland; and Cedd and his brothers at Lastingham. The virtues Bede saw in the Irish monks seemed to indicate to him that at last there was hope for the Irish schismatics, and the problem they had posed to the Church from the beginning of his account. Such virtues and miracles as theirs must, Bede suggests, eventually be linked into the unity of the Church by acceptance of the calculation most generally followed for the celebration of the feast of the Resurrection. The central chapter of this book and of the whole work, therefore, recounts the debate at the Synod of Whitby in which the question of the date of Easter was officially resolved for Northumbria. Significantly, the decision was reached not by an evaluation of evidence but by an affirmation of allegiance and a concern for personal salvation at the last:

> The king said . . . 'I intend to obey his [St Peter's] commands in everything to the best of my knowledge and ability, otherwise when I come to the gates of the kingdom of heaven, there may be no-one to open them'.[20]

Extended missions, new dioceses, monastic vocations, monastic foundations, as well as political and military successes and setbacks overcome, form the web of this central and packed book. Moreover, the rest of the saints in the seventh age is seen as already affecting the life of the island; miracles, the sign of the work of God among men, abound, especially in the place of the burial of the saints. A living man, Fursa, an Irish hermit, recounted a dream-vision which Bede thought worth including at length in his work, adding that the longer written account he was summarizing would also repay study. The other world was opened to the new Christians here and now, and the promises of God, for both condemnation and redemption, were illustrated in the experience of contemporaries.

The last chapter, like those of the previous books, presented another way in which Christianity faced disaster. The disaster, this time of plague, had two results, not one: Sebbi of the East Saxons prayed but Sigehere, with whom he ruled jointly, apostastized. The last sentences of the book reveal the repentance and second acceptance of faith by Sigehere and his people as a new stage in understanding by the Anglo-Saxons of providence and politics:

They chose rather to die believing that they would rise again in him than to live in the filth of unbelief among their idols.[21]

BOOK FOUR

Book Four at once presents a new and positive stage in the conversion of the English with the appointment of a Greek, Theodore of Tarsus, as archbishop of Canterbury, with his companion, the learned and saintly Hadrian from Africa. Theodore was the archbishop of Bede's youth: he was consecrated archbishop of Canterbury before Bede was born and died the year before he was made deacon. For Bede, Theodore and Hadrian were a living contact for the English Church with the Mediterranean world and Rome, but even more through their learning with the tradition of the Fathers. With them, the possibilities in England for learning were vastly increased; in this 'fourth age' of maturity for the English, language of many kinds was thriving in a new way:

> Because both of them were extremely learned in sacred and secular literature, they attracted a crowd of students into whose minds they daily poured the streams of wholesome learning.[22]

They taught also 'the art of metre, astronomy, and ecclesiastical computation',[23] the subjects Bede himself learned and taught in Jarrow. They expanded learning particularly by instruction in Bede's two languages, Greek as well as Latin. The musical tradition of the Church already established now flourished everywhere: 'the knowledge of sacred music began to be taught in all the English churches'. Already, as Bede made clear elsewhere, the liturgical tradition of chant was known in Kent at both Canterbury and Rochester, by the work of both Eddius Stephanus, a monk of Canterbury, and Putta, the bishop of Rochester, who was 'especially skilled in liturgical chanting after the Roman manner'. This tradition was carried to the north, not by Theodore but during his episcopate, by Bishop Wilfrid, who took Eddius Stephanus, later his biographer, to teach music at Ripon, while in 680 the monasteries of Jarrow and Wearmouth received John the archchanter of St Peter's in Rome, brought from there by Benedict Biscop, just after Bede became a member of the Wearmouth community: John 'taught the cantors of the monastery the order and manner of singing and reading aloud' and invited musicians from other monasteries to to join his school.[24] The preoccupation of the first missionaries with conversion, baptism and preaching was over, the Church was established and under Theodore's rule reached the 'fourth age of maturity'. Monasteries, among them Wearmouth and Jarrow, were flourishing on English soil; Hilda had chosen to become a nun in England, Wilfrid had a thriving monastery at Ripon, while Colman had attempted to establish a joint Anglo-Irish monastery on the island of Inishbofin. He had quickly discovered a profound incompatibility between the Irish and English members of his foundation, a matter not of theology but of temperament:

> They could not agree together because the Irish, in summertime when the harvest had to be gathered in, left the monastery and wandered about, scattering into various places with which they were familiar; then when winter came, they returned and expected to have a share in the things which the English had provided.[25]

Christian education was now able to take firm root in the schools of Canterbury, East Anglia and at Jarrow itself. Synods were held at Hertford and Hatfield to resolve matters of discipline and agree on matters of doctrine. The outskirts of the island received the faith with the conversion of the Isle of Wight by Beornwine, the nephew of Bishop Wilfrid, and the priest Hiddila; there the death of two princes gave the place what to Bede was the sure foundation for faith, martyrdom. Heaven opened to receive the saints, such as the nuns of Barking, Bishop Chad, Queen Aethelthryth and Abbess Hilda, and to bestow the gift of Christian poetry on Caedmon, the cowherd of Whitby.

However great the gifts of God to the English as recorded in Book Four, the end of this book, like the others, contains also severe judgements from heaven, one monastic, the other secular. The abbey of Coldingham, where Cuthbert had visited the royal abbess Aebbe, was burned down after a warning from the Irish penitent Adamnan who stayed there and learned in a dream that no-one in the monastery was seriously committed to their calling;

> Men and women alike are sunk in slothful slumbers or else they remain awake for the purposes of sin. And the cells that were built for praying and for reading have become haunts of feasting, drinking, gossip and other delights.[26]

It was a warning Bede says he had recorded for his own times, when, as he later wrote to Egbert of York, monastic life had been even more eroded.

The second disaster occurred in 684, when King Ecgfrith of Northumbria, the patron of Wearmouth and Jarrow and the husband of Queen Aethelthryth, was killed during a rash campaign against the Picts, which Bede described as a just punishment for his unprovoked attack on Ireland, where he had burned churches and monasteries and provoked the inhabitants to curse him. In both cases the message is the same: external profession of Christianity was not enough; religious and kings alike stood under the judgement of God. It was the beginning of the last and fifth period, the old age of the world, and Bede commented, 'From this time the strength of the English kingdom began to ebb and fall away'.[27] In the south also, in 685, King Hlothere of Kent, a nephew of Queen Aethelthryth, was killed by the hand of his nephew Eadric and after Eadric's death eighteen months later, 'various usurpers and foreign kings plundered the kingdom', until the accession of Wihtred in 690.

But to this familiar ending in defeat and judgement, Bede had a story to add of outstanding glory and encouragement on another plane: the last chapters of Book Four are a summary of the life of Cuthbert of Lindisfarne. The year of Ecgfrith's death gave Bede the chance to refer to it also as the year in which that king had 'caused Cuthbert to be consecrated as bishop of Lindisfarne'. He then gave an admirable summary of the saint, based, as he says, on his previous accounts in verse and in prose but here adapted to present the ideal picture of the man of God, to encourage where his previous examples had warned.

Cuthbert is here described first of all as the ideal monk and prior, an Englishman taught by the gentle Eata and the devout Boisil, in the monastery established by Irish monks at Melrose, learning from them, by their words and by their deeds, to know the Scriptures. Then he is described as the ideal pastor, both as monk and then as bishop, riding or walking to reach 'the villages that were far away on steep and rugged mountains', preaching, hearing confessions, weeping with compunction when he celebrated the Eucharist, spending his time in 'works of virtue like those of the apostles'. His days of 'silence and secrecy' as a hermit proved to be not a contrast to but a continuation of his life as a disciple of Christ, and when Bede described his return to the active apostolate as bishop, he says 'he held that to give the weak brethren help and advice was a fit substitute for prayer' which Bede linked with the two commandments of love (Matthew 22:36, 39). Cuthbert's death was accompanied by prophecy, and Bede here adds two accounts of miracles which had taken place in connection with the incorrupt body of the saint, which he had recently heard about: Baduthegn, guest-master of Lindisfarne in Bede's day, said that he had been cured of a sudden paralysis while praying and sleeping by the tomb of Cuthbert; a young man told Bede how he had been cured of a tumour on his eye by the touch of a hair from the head of Cuthbert which Thrythred, the abbot of a monastery on the Dacre, kept in a casket. The mysterious and severe judgements of God over the English were thus seen as tempered with mercy and hope.

BOOK FIVE

The first chapter of Book Five links it with the previous book by an account of Oethewald, the successor of Cuthbert as a hermit on Farne, and a miracle connected with him told to Bede by its recipient, Guthfrith of Lindisfarne. By describing the death of Oethewald in the reign of Aldfrith, Bede then turns the narrative smoothly back to the reign of that king in Northumbria and then proceeds to draw together the original themes of the whole work and at the same time to indicate the wider horizons that were now open for the English in their 'fifth age'.

The bishop-heroes of this book are John of Hexham (d. 721), who had ordained Bede as deacon and as priest, and Wilfrid of York, whom Bede had also met. The account of Bishop John is warm and lively: in it John is seen as uniting the orthodox faith of the Roman mission with the virtues of the Irish. He is first described as withdrawing, like the Irish monks, with his companions to fast and pray in solitude during Lent. While there, John continued his pastoral care to both the poor and the sick, in a series of vivid and humane incidents, thus also fulfilling his duty as a bishop. The northern-born John was a local saint for Bede, being buried at Beverley, only ten years before Bede finished his history. In recording the death of Bishop Wilfrid in 709, Bede reviewed the events of the life of one of the most outstanding of the English bishops, and the one most deeply involved in the life of the wider Church. Bede summarized a fuller account written by Eddius Stephanus, and while it is entirely correct and respectful in its praise of Wilfrid there is a lack of spontaneity about it which suggests that Bede had little personal sympathy with this able statesman-prelate.[28]

Book Five also demonstrates that the English Church had not only its own saints but its own learned clergy, in Tobias (d. 726), the new bishop of Rochester, 'a man of great learning', as well as the new archbishop of Canterbury, Albinus, the 'only-begetter' of the *Ecclesiastical History* itself. Both were men learned in Latin and Greek as well as Saxon; with them the Church was established, and interpreters were no longer needed. Moreover, the English Church was now open towards pagan Europe, and the first missions of the English are described, by Wihtberht who went, as well as Willibrord, to preach to the heathen in Frisia, and the two brothers, Hewald the White and Hewald the Black, who proposed to go on a mission of conversion to Old Saxony. This preaching was supported not only by prayer but also by martrydom: Hewald the White was killed by the sword and Hewald the Black tortured to death before they reached their destination and both were buried in Cologne, where miracles illustrated their sanctity.[29]

Nor were the missionaries the only ones to go outside the island: in Book Five, Bishop Wilfrid is described as a constant visitor to Rome and three kings and a prince are praised for leaving their kingdoms to go to Rome: Caedwalla and Ine of the West Saxons and Cenred of Mercia with Ceolred son of Aethelred. All chose to die at the threshold of the apostles.

Other parts of this earth were not the only places now open to the Anglo-Saxons: saints continued to pass through into heaven and that other world was now also open through visions to the English as well as the Irish. The Englishman Egbert who while living in Ireland formed a plan to go and convert the heathen in Germany was persuaded to go instead to 'the monasteries of Columba' by repeated dreams not of apostolic or angelic persons but the much more recent Boisil of Melrose. While Book Three had contained the vision of the Irish monk Fursa, in Book Four there is a long account of a dream-visit to heaven and hell, this time by Drythelm, the devout married man of Northumbria who became a monk and solitary at Melrose after his terrifying journeys in a dream through the next world. There he saw two aspects of the sixth age of the dead: there was a 'flowery place', full of joyful people awaiting their ultimate entry into heaven, but there was also a place of 'awful flaming fire and freezing cold' which was the entrance to the pit of hell, where Drythelm saw 'bishops, priests and women' among that 'countless multitude of misshapen souls'. Such stern visions were not confined to Drythelm: a thane of King Cenred of Mercia died in despair, after a wicked life without repentance. He had dreamed beforehand of a small and light book of his good deeds and a large heavy book of his sins and knew himself damned. In Bede's own monastery he remembered a monk-blacksmith who, in spite of a dream of 'the place of everlasting damnation' prepared for him, refused to repent and died in sin. These instances included in Book Five provided Bede with an opportunity for warning the living and he adds

> This happened lately in the kingdom of Bernicia. The story spread far and wide and roused many people to do penance for their sins without delay. And may the reading of this account of ours have the same effect.[30]

In the fifth age there was still more need for urgent realization of the responsibilities that growing old in the faith had brought. The last days of the world, the sixth age, might come to an end at any time, and Bede's final book included these dark warnings to be on the watch. But the book ends on a positive note with the final unity of the Church established, especially with a notable victory in the matter of the Easter question. Bede included a letter of Ceolfrith to the Scots on the subject of the calculation of time, centred on Easter, in which the arguments Bede himself had clarified elsewere were again set out. Even Iona, the heart of Celtic monasticism and the home of Aidan, Colman and the rest, now accepted the Catholic calculation of Easter. The problem that was first stated in Book One, of the reconciliation of those Christians in the British Isles who were in this matter outside the unity of the Church, was thus seen to have been resolved. The state of England, now united to the Christ of the resurrection, was one, potentially, of peace and love. Creation had found its fulfilment in re-creation through baptism, and the paradise was, or at least could be beginning to be, restored, though even in this paragraph Bede had his warning to add: 'What the result will be a later generation will discover'.[31]

THE LETTER TO EGBERT

Bede's account of the English race was not a partial and prejudiced national history shot through with naïve idealism but a piece of great historical theology. It was a carefully structured account of one period of time, in one place, in which people and events were viewed in the perspective of eternity. It was not a mythical account but based on facts which were as accurate as it was possible for Bede to make them, and for that reason an amazing amount of information about Anglo-Saxon England has been extracted from it, most of it supported by other evidence. The facts again and again have proved reliable; Bede was a keen observer with a good judgement, which he applied to the history of his own race as carefully as he did to the pages of the Scriptures.

It was not, however, Bede's purpose to provide a mine of facts for future historians but to assist the conversion of his readers. The *Ecclesiastical History* was concerned with the present and an appendix to it was formed by Bede's comments on his own times, the sixth age of the world, in his letter to Egbert of York. Bede had sent his *History* to King Ceolwulf for a specific purpose, as part of his life's work for the conversion of England, 'for the instruction of yourself and those over whom divine authority has appointed you to rule'.[32] He described the king as a helper for Archbishop Egbert, his cousin, in the task of reform before him.[33]

In 733 Bede had made one of his rare visits outside his monastery and gone to York, already sick, perhaps with the illness of which he was soon to die. He had talked with his former pupil about the actual problems and real difficulties of the Church in England in the 730s, and his letter replaced the further comments he would have made had he been well enough to undertake the second visit they had planned. It was a challenging and outspoken letter, full of stern condemnation for hypocrisy and urgent advice to the bishop as the person responsible before God for the English clergy and people in the last age. The *Ecclesiastical History* had given, in the form of vivid examples, the same message to King Ceolwulf that Bede set out in his letter to the king's cousin, Egbert of York. In the *History* Bede had shown how the blessing of God rests upon those who follow the apostolic example and commands, instead of their own self-seeking. In the letter he described the clergy as often lax and greedy, failing

> not only to preach the Gospel freely and lay their hands on the faithful, but even which is more serious, after accepting money from their hearers, which was forbidden by our Lord, they despise the ministry of the Word which the Lord ordered them to perform.[34]

They neglected especially

> the villages and hamlets of our people which are situated in inaccessible mountains and dense woodlands.[35]

In the *History* Bede had shown that ideal for pastors, Cuthbert, performing just these forms of ministry in poverty and zeal, a saint and an apostle for all to imitate, a perfect type of Christ. Where Bede deplores in the letter the increase in the false monasteries, where no monastic life was lived at all, in the 30 years 'since King Aldfrith was removed from earthly things', in the *History* he had given both the example of Whitby and the warning of Coldingham to rebuke the same vice. It was a letter filled with urgent warnings about the state of the English Church in the sixth age of the world, the old age of its weakness and senility.

THE CHRONICLES

At the end of the *Ecclesiastical History* Bede gave a brief summary of his own life and a list of his works, and then gave as an 'aid to memory', a summary of dates and events, in the manner of a chronologer. This was not his first piece of chronological writing. Before the *Ecclesiastical History* was begun, he had put together two chronicles, the *Chronica Maiora* and the shorter *Chronica Minora*, each part of other didactic works. Some of the material in them Bede later incorporated into his other writings, and each contains an explanation of the dating of Easter. Like other chronicles, the dates listed were followed by shorter or longer descriptive entries of events and people, a record rather than an interpretive piece of history like the *Ecclesiastical History*. Bede's *History* is essentially concerned with the aspect of life in Anglo-Saxon England which related to the conversion of a people to Christianity and it has therefore more in common with the biblical commentaries than with the chronicles. But they have one thing in common and that is the structure of the ages of the world. The shorter chronicle in particular ends, like the *History*, in expectation of future mysteries; the extent of the final age, the sixth age leading to the end of all things, it asserts, is 'clear only in the sight of God'.[36]

Another factor distinguished the *History* from the chronicles. Like the commentaries, the *Ecclesiastical History of the English People* included both exhortations to the reader and the personal prayers of the writer, notably at the beginning and at the end. At the end of the Preface, Bede asks prayers from his readers:

> Furthermore, I humbly beseech all who either read this history of our nation or hear it read, that they will not forget to ask for God's mercy frequently upon my weakness of both mind and body.[37]

At the end he wrote

And I pray you, merciful Jesus, that as you have graciously
granted me sweet draughts from the Word which tells of you,
so you will of your goodness grant that I may come at length
to you, the fountain of all wisdom, and stand before your face
forever.[38]

In both cases, Bede was acknowledging his own place within the
sweep of redemptive history which he had presented to his readers.
He had not been concerned with the history of the English Church,
as of an institution distinguishable from other English institutions,
such as the English monarchy or the English army, but the ecclesiastical dimension of all aspects of the English people. He had restruc-
tured the accounts they had of their immediate past to give it
meaning by discerning the action of God within the whole. It was a
book for secular men, including rulers, and its aim was that of all
Bede's writing: the conversion of the reader, so that by reading or
hearing what God had already done for his nation, he might

eschew what is harmful and perverse and . . . with greater care
pursue those things which he had learned to be good and
pleasing in the sight of God.[39]

Notes

1   HE, V.23, p. 561.

2   Augustine, *Expositions on the Psalms*, trans. A. C. Coxe (repr.
    Michigan, 1979), *Psalm* 96(97):3, p. 475.

3   Ibid., *Psalm* 29(30):5, p. 67.

4   *Homilies* II, 9, pp. 240-1.

5   HE, Preface, p. 3.

6   Cf. R. W. Southern, *Aspects of European Historical Writing* (Royal
    Historical Society Presidential Address, 1975) for an illuminating
    discussion of this topic.

7   *Luke* 11:26-34, p. 67.

8   Jerome, *On the Perpetual Virginity of Blessed Mary against Helvidius*,
    1 (PL 23, 187-8). For discussion of *verax historicus* cf. C. W. Jones,
    Saints' Lives and Chronicles (Ithaca, NY, 1947), p. 83, note 7; R. Ray,
    'Bede's *vera lex historiae*', *Speculum* 55 (1980), 1-21 and in *Famulus
    Christi*, pp. 125-41.

9   *Chronica Minora*, DT XVI, pp. 600-1. For discussion of this theme in
    later literature see J. A. Burrows, *The Ages of Man: a Study in
    Medieval Writing and Thought* (Oxford, 1988).

10   This connection between the five books of the *Ecclesiastical History* and the five books of the Pentateuch was examined by Dr Henry Mayr-Harting in his Latin Sermon to the University of Oxford in 1981.

11   HE, I.1, p. 15.

12   Ibid. I.22, p. 69.

13   Ibid. II.1, pp. 123–35; cf. *The Earliest Life of Gregory the Great by a Monk of Whitby*, ed. and trans. B. Colgrave (University of Kansas, Lawrence, Kansas, 1968). For a recent discussion of this *Life* see Sean Mosford, 'The Whitby Life of Pope Gregory', unpublished Oxford thesis, 1988.

14   HE, II.2, p. 141.

15   Ibid., II.6, p. 155.

16   Ibid., II.13, p. 183.

17   Ibid., II.16, p. 193.

18   Ibid., III.1, p. 213.

19   Ibid., III.17, p. 267.

20   Ibid., III.25, p. 307.

21   Ibid., III.30, p. 323.

22   Ibid., IV.2, p. 333.

23   Ibid.

24   Ibid., IV.8, p. 380. Cf. HA, 6, p. 190.

25   Ibid., IV.4, pp. 347–9.

26   Ibid., IV.25, pp. 425–7.

27   Ibid., IV.25, p. 429.

28   Ibid., V.19, pp. 517–31. Cf. Eddius Stephanus, *The Life of Bishop Wilfrid*, ed. and trans. B. Colgrave (Cambridge, 1926).

29   Ibid., V.10, pp. 481–3.

30   Ibid., V.14, p. 505.

31   Ibid., V.23, p. 561.

32   Ibid., Preface, p. 3.

33   *Letter to Egbert* (Whitelock), p. 739.

34   Ibid., p. 738.

35   Ibid.

36   DT, 17.219. I owe this insight to Dr R. Marcus, *Bede and the Tradition of Ecclesiastical History* (Jarrow Lecture, 1975), p. 15.

37   HE, Preface, p. 7.

38   Ibid., V.24, p. 571.

39   Ibid., Preface, p. 3.

6

Bede's influence

On 13 November 1899 Pope Leo XIII issued a proclamation through the Sacred Congregation of Rites authorizing the celebration of the Office and Mass of St Bede the Venerable as a Doctor of the universal Church.[1] The first and only Englishman to be acclaimed as *doctor ecclesiae*, Bede was now counted among the Fathers he had so reverenced and followed. Previously, his feast had been kept in the Benedictine and Cistercian Orders with solemnity and affection; now he was formally recognized as both saint and teacher not only for the English but for all Christians. Such a sign of respect was therefore no innovation but a recognition of a long-existing fact.

THE DEATH OF BEDE

Bede's sanctity has always been seen as intimately bound up with his work as a Christian scholar, as he would himself have wished. The earliest description of Bede as a saint came from Jarrow and was an account of his death by his pupil Cuthbert, who became abbot of Jarrow fifteen years later. He described Bede as a scholar to the end; his death was the passing of 'God's chosen servant, Bede, our father and master'. In his last illness, 'daily he gave us lessons who were his pupils . . . we read and wept by turns'. He continued:

> During those days there were two pieces of work worthy of record, besides the lessons he gave us every day and his chant-ing of the psalter, which he desired to finish: the gospel of John

134

which he was turning into our mother-tongue to the great profit of the church, from the beginning as far as the words 'But what are they among so many?' (John 1:1 – 6:9) and a selection from Bishop Isidore's book *On the Wonders of Nature*, for he said, 'I cannot have my children learning what is not true and losing their labour on this after I have gone'.[2]

The themes of learning and teaching in Bede's life continued to the end, like another great monastic scholar who died in England four centuries later, Anselm of Canterbury.[3] But neither Anselm nor Bede was just an assiduous teacher, like Browning's *Grammarian*, who 'decided not to live but know'. As well as his learning, Abbot Cuthbert emphasized Bede's human qualities, his joy, thankfulness and prayerfulness, his simplicity and poverty, his humility and his peacefulness. He died after quoting the words Paulinus had recorded of Ambrose, one of Bede's favourites among the Fathers of the Church,

> I have not so lived that life among you as would now make me ashamed; but I am not afraid to die either, for the God we serve is good.[4]

Abbot Cuthbert described his passing with the same imagery as that used by Bede himself for so many saintly deaths:

> Because he always laboured here most devoutly in the praise of God, his soul was borne by angels to the long-desired delights of heaven.

It was intended as more than a pious hope; it was an affirmation of the direct entry into heaven of one Cuthbert had known well for many years and believed to be a saint.

Other letters of Abbot Cuthbert contained eulogies of Bede, urging wider veneration for him than that offered by his own monastery:

> It seems fitting to me that the whole nation of the English wherever they are found should thank God that he gave them within their nation so marvellous a man, endowed with various gifts, and so zealous in exercising his gifts and likewise living in a virtuous manner.[5]

It was Bede's own preferred virtues that Abbot Cuthbert praised, rather than instances of more dramatic sanctity, a low-key and monastic profile of interest to those who had known Benedict Biscop, Ceolfrith and Sigehere of Wearmouth–Jarrow, rather than the devotees of miracle-workers such as Guthlac, the wonder-working hermit of Crowland (d. 714). Only one miracle was connected with Bede, either during his life or after his death: Alcuin of York, in his poem on *The Saints of the Church of York*, mentioned an otherwise unattested cure after Bede's death; he called it 'a miraculous act of healing':

> When a sick man was surrounded by the relics of that blessed father he was completely cured from his illness.[6]

EARLY VENERATION IN EUROPE

The fact that Bede was accounted a saint by his contemporaries at Jarrow does not seem to have ensured that he would be equally venerated immediately elsewhere in England, though Abbot Cuthbert continued to publicize his sanctity. It was not to a colleague in England but to Boniface, the Anglo-Saxon apostle of Frisia and Germany (c. 675–754), then in Mainz, that he wrote with gratitude for

> a cloth all of silk for the relics of Bede, our teacher of blessed memory to serve for the perpetuation and veneration of him.[7]

No evidence survives of a liturgical cult of Bede in eighth-century England. Perhaps this was partly because he died on 26 May, already the day on which Augustine of Canterbury was celebrated as a saint. When his name was later inserted in English calendars, it appears either after that of Augustine, as a commemoration rather than a feast in its own right, or on the next day. It was outside England that the fame of Bede flourished, returning to England with the foreign influence on the monastic revival, which also aroused a renewed instinct for the Anglo-Saxon past. This recognition of Bede as a saint on the Continent was indissolubly linked with Bede as a writer. Respect for Bede's writings had grown up abroad during his lifetime and all his works were copied and distributed abroad. His writings circulated widely and with them went Abbot Cuthbert's account of the death of Bede.

Two English men abroad were especially responsible for the spread of Bede's works. His contemporary, Boniface, wrote urgently to Jarrow asking for works of Bede to help him in the missionary work he had undertaken in Frisia, calling Bede 'a candle of the church which the Holy Spirit has illuminated'. In 746/7, he wrote again, now as archbishop of Mainz, to Egbert of York:

I beg you also to have copied and sent to me some of the treatises of the lector Bede, whom, as we learn, divine grace endowed with spiritual intelligence and permitted to shine forth in your country, so that we too may profit by the light of the torch which the Lord has granted you.[8]

A little later in a letter to Hwaetberht, abbot of Wearmouth, he was more specific in his requests:

We beg you to be so kind as to copy and send us some of the treatises of that keen investigator of the Scriptures, the monk Bede, who we have learned, shone forth among you of late as a lantern in the church by his scriptural scholarship.[9]

Later still he wrote again to Hwaetberht:

Send us some spark from the light of the church which the Holy Spirit has kindled in your land; namely that you will be so kind as to send us some portion of the treatises which Bede, that inspired priest and student of the Sacred Scriptures, has put forth in his writings. Most especially if possible his lectionary for the year which would form a convenient and useful manual for us in our preaching and the Proverbs of Solomon since we hear he has written some commentaries on this book.[10]

Such popularity was not expected at Jarrow and in 763/4, Abbot Cuthbert wrote to Lul, the companion and eventually the successor of Boniface (c. 710–786), mentioning the difficulties found in his monastery in answering this unparalleled demand for copies of their famous author:

Now truly since you have asked me for some of the works of the blessed father [Bede], out of love for you, I have prepared what I could with my pupils according to our strength. I have sent in accordance with your wishes the books about the man of God, Cuthbert, composed in verse and prose. And if I could have done more, I would gladly have done so. The conditions of the past winter oppressed the island of our race very horribly with cold and ice and long and widespread storms of wind and rain, so that the hand of the scribe was hindered from producing a great number of books.[11]

Times had not changed since Bede himself had to act as scribe for copies of his own works.[12] But the demand was remorseless: twenty years later Lul was writing in a similar vein to Aethelberht of York:

I beg you to acquire and kindly send us any of those books which the priest Bede of blessed memory composed, for our consolation in our exile; mainly four books on the first part of Samuel as far as the death of Saul and three books on Ezra and Nehemiah and four books on the Gospel of St Mark. Perhaps I make heavy demands but I enjoin nothing heavy to true love.[13]

It has been plausibly suggested, from the use of an insular minuscule hand in two surviving manuscripts of Bede in Germany, that the demand for Bede's work abroad caused a change in handwriting at Wearmouth–Jarrow, a further indication of both the popularity of his works overseas and the lack of extra copies in his own monastery.[14]

For the second of Bede's English influential admirers abroad, Alcuin of York (c. 735–804), the architect of the Carolingian renaissance, his influence was all-pervasive. Alcuin was trained in York in the school set up and administered by Bede's pupil Egbert, and taught by Aethelberht; Bede was his 'master', 'the most notable teacher of our age'.[15] In his letters he praised Bede, recommended his life as a model for monks and sent copies of his works to his friends. In his poem on *The Saints of the Church of York* he drew two-thirds of the material from Bede's *Ecclesiastical History* and his *Life of St Cuthbert*, with 30 lines devoted to an account of Bede's life, works, death and a miracle. After recording Bede's entry into the monastery (here anachronistically called Jarrow, in fact at the time, Wearmouth) he comments first on Bede's good life in an extended paraphrase of Bede's own account of himself praising his diligence and wisdom as a scholar:

Wise even as a youth, he was always keen and eager
To learn or to write working with unfailing diligence and such
was his progress that he was made a teacher as he deserved.

Alcuin then lists those of Bede's works which had most influenced him, putting the commentaries on Scripture first:

This famous scholar wrote many works,
Unravelling the mysterious volumes of Holy Scripture
And composed a handbook on the art of metre.
He also wrote with marvellous clarity a book on time
containing the courses, places, times and laws of the stars.
He was the author in lucid prose of books on history,
and composer of many poems in the metrical style.

138

He concludes with Bede's familiar phrase about his biblical commentaries: 'He followed the footsteps of the ancient fathers'.[16] Bede's treatises were the manuals of Alcuin's school at the court of Charlemagne and therefore have a strong claim to be regarded as the formative influence on the West in the early Middle Ages.

THE CULT OF BEDE IN ENGLAND

The monastery of Jarrow was destroyed by Viking attacks early in the ninth century and remained deserted until the eleventh century. Bede's fame, however, was not linked exclusively with his monastery. The English monasteries involved in the monastic reforms of the tenth century regarded Bede as an outstanding predecessor and honoured him accordingly: his name was included in calendars from New Minster and Winchester, Worcester and Evesham, Sherbourne, and by the fourteenth century from Canterbury, Exeter and Hereford.[17] Wulfstan of Worcester (c. 1008–95) had a particular regard for Bede. Not only is he mentioned in the sanctorale, homilary, passional, psalter and antiphonal in the *Book of Wulfstan* but in 1062 Wulfstan's first act after his consecration as bishop was to dedicate a church to Bede in Worcester:

> On the morrow of his consecration, he dedicated a church to blessed Bede. Rightly did he begin by dedicating a church to him whose name stands first in English letters. That day he watered the people with so flowing a discourse that none might doubt that Wulfstan was inspired by the Holy Spirit with the same eloquence that of old had moved the tongue of Bede.[18]

The voice is the voice of Wulfstan but the hands are perhaps those of his biographer William of Malmesbury (c. 1080–1143). Wulfstan may well have built the chapel as described, but the tone in which admiration for Bede is expressed is that of the monastic scholar and historian and not of the pastorally-minded bishop. In the third book of his *Gesta Pontificum* William expressed his admiration for Bede in similar terms and built upon his account of early English history as upon an unshakeable source. It was an historian, rather than a bishop, who appreciated another historian and used his works.

Devotion to Bede expanded in England in the eleventh century and instead of being focused on Jarrow, it emerged in Durham. In the late eleventh century, the author of the *History of the Church of Durham* says that

139

in honour of this Bede a porch is consecrated in the northern side of the church of St Paul at Jarrow and reminds the people of his venerable name.[19]

The author of this account, the climax of which is the reintroduction of monks in the 1090s into the cathedral, supplied information about Bede's body. He says that he had been buried at Jarrow but later his bones were stolen and removed to Durham. It is a strange story and deserves some consideration in detail. Stories seem to have circulated in Durham about a certain eccentric clergyman, Alfred Westou, a married priest attached to the church which housed the body of Cuthbert in Durham in the mid-eleventh century. He was said, rather curiously, to have been held in respect by 'the lovers of what is honest and God-fearing', acting as a severe preceptor to the boys of the cathedral, while stealing relics of the northern saints from their shrines and exhibiting a hair from the head of Cuthbert, which continually emerged whole after he had set it alight. Tradition was also alleged to have said that he was responsible for conveying the bones of Bede to the cathedral:

It was his custom ... annually to visit the monastery of Jarrow, in which as he knew the doctor Bede had lived, died and was buried, near the anniversary of the day of his death and there to pray and keep vigil. Once he went there as usual and after having spent some days in the church alone in prayer and vigil, very early in the morning he returned alone to Durham, something he had never done before. .... Although he lived for many years after this, he never again troubled himself to visit the monastery of Jarrow but conducted himself like a person who had what he desires. When he was asked by his close friends where was the resting place of the bones of the venerable Bede, his usual answer, given with the promptness of a man who knows what he is saying, was, 'No-one knows better about this than I do. Dearly beloved, consider this something firmly and certainly established: that the same shrine which contains the most holy body of the father Cuthbert contains also the bones of the teacher and monk Bede. Let no-one seek for any portion of his relics outside the covering of this shrine.'

Alfred Westou then warned his hearers not to talk about this, for a reason which directly suggests the tradition of theft of relics: silence should be observed

lest strangers resident in the church should plot treachery, for it was their most ardent wish to carry off if it were possible the relics of the saints and chiefly those of Bede.[20]

It may be that all this was indeed part of the oral tradition at Durham, but the close similarities should not be overlooked between this unedifying tale and the mediaeval literary genre of the 'pious theft' story. For many reasons, varying from devotion to a saint to the need for the income brought by pilgrims, relics were often stolen throughout the Middle Ages and taken from one shrine to another. But what was most important about such a theft was not the fact but the story that went with it. At times, it is clear that a story would be elaborated without any actual theft at all and a 'tradition' invented, explaining that some relics had been taken secretly from a deserted shrine and reburied in the place where the story was told. This would increase the glory of the new shrine at the expense of the old. All the most common elements of this tradition are there in the story told about Alfred Westou: the pious pilgrim, the neglected grave, the theft in secret by night, the reburial in a shrine which was later eager to collect the relics of northern saints. It is at least possible that this story was invented at Durham in the eleventh century to give an aura of ancient tradition to their claim to the presence of the bones of Bede in the cathedral beside those of Cuthbert about whom he had written so much. The story may well have been attached to Westou, since he was already known to have been obsessed by Cuthbert and relics.

Outside evidence for the theft is lacking and a rumour about Alfred Westou seems a dubious basis for assertions of fact. The story was first written down a hundred years after the supposed event and additional support for this tale was later still. The story appeared first in a piece of writing directed to the glory of the shrine of Cuthbert and culminating in the account of the monastic community created at Durham with monks from Jarrow in 1083. Two pieces of 'supporting' evidence given by William of Malmesbury in the twelfth century were both derived from the same Durham account. First, the eleventh-century author says, and William repeats him as saying, that the presence of the bones of Bede near Cuthbert was referred to in an Anglo-Saxon poem; this poem seems to have been written around 1100, long after the arrival of the new monks in Durham. Secondly, they both say that a bag containing the bones of Bede was found in the coffin of Cuthbert when it was opened in 1106. The fact that the small bag of bones was found there in the twelfth century does not prove that Westou put them there in the eleventh.

The story of Alfred Westou was confused rather than confirmed later by Reginald of Durham, a monk who wrote about the post-humous miracles of Cuthbert *c.* 1104. In order to remove some problems from the story of Alfred Westou in *The History of the Church of Durham*, he described Alfred as the custodian of the shrine of Cuthbert, concerned with combing the saint's hair and trimming his nails, a story found in connection with other saints, for instance Osmund of Salisbury. He included a story about Cuthbert and a mother-weasel which has been shown to be a piece of propaganda rather than a record of fact. It may be that Reginald, as he claims, heard this story also from the great-grandson of Alfred Westou, Aelred, the saintly abbot of Rievaulx, to whom he dedicated his account of Cuthbert's miracles; but in the writings of Aelred himself and of his biographer this story is completely lacking. Even if Reginald did hear this from Aelred, the source remains the highly imaginative rumours about an early devotee of northern sanctity, remembered by either the community at Durham, or the family of one of its members. The story of Alfred Westou, therefore, rests on the late eleventh-century account alone. Finally, if the relics of Bede had been taken to Durham in the 1090s, the translation failed in its purpose. There was no public confirmation of the event at Durham; Bede's name was not included in any calendar drawn up at Durham before 1170; his feast became part of the liturgical life of Durham only in the thirteenth century.

In the eleventh century, between 1072 and 1074, English monks returned to Jarrow.[21] Their leader was Aldwin, a monk from Winchcombe in Gloucestershire, inspired in the venture by reading the works of Bede, and with him went Reinfrid, a northerner, who had grieved over the desolation he saw at the site of the abbey of Whitby, and Aelfwig, a deacon, both from the monastery of Evesham. They settled at Jarrow and others joined them; attempts were made to refound Wearmouth and Melrose also. But in 1083, the monks were brought by William of St Calais to Durham and became the first members of Durham Cathedral priory, one of the most famous religious houses in England throughout the Middle Ages. They continued to provide one or two monks at Jarrow, as at Wearmouth and on Holy Island, but effectively the tradition of Bede had been transferred to Durham. It is possible that it was at this moment that the relics of Bede were brought to Durham, since so much of the tradition about them appeared at that time.

142

When Hugh Pudsey was bishop of Durham (1153–95) the bones of Bede were taken from the coffin of Cuthbert and placed in a reliquary nearby; in 1370, they were removed to the Galilee Chapel, where they were venerated until the shrine was destroyed at the Reformation. A large marble slab was then placed over the place where the shrine had stood, with the inscription *Hac sunt in fossa Bedae venerabilis ossa* ('Here in this grave are the bones of the Venerable Bede'). An examination of the grave under the slab in 1830 revealed some human bones in the remains of a coffin, perhaps reburied in the sixteenth century. In the twentieth century, the dean of Durham, Dean Allington, placed a memorial on the wall behind the slab with words from Bede's commentary on Revelation:

> Christ is the morning star who when the night of this world is past brings to his saints the promise of the light of life and opens everlasting day.[22]

BEDE AS A GREAT CHRISTIAN THINKER

In the twelfth century Amalarius of Metz referred to Bede as an indisputable authority: 'for me his authority is sufficient'.[23] In the thirteenth, Thomas Aquinas quoted Bede with approval, particularly for his views on cosmology.[24] In the fifteenth, Cardinal Bellarmine proposed, in a phrase quoted in Leo XIII's document recognizing Bede as a Doctor of the Church, that 'Bede has illuminated the West, Damasus the East',[25] a comparison which suggests that Bede was then seen as much more than an historian of the Church.

What in the works of Bede has left a lasting mark on human history? In what sense can he be classed as a 'great Christian thinker'? If it is necessary to see 'great Christian thinkers' only as those who have contributed towards pushing forwards the boundaries of theological and philosophical thinking about doctrine, Bede would hardly qualify; he had no new speculations to propose about God or salvation, though he understood very clearly and taught with immense ability what was already established. But if the term 'Christian thinker' can be expanded in the way Anselm of Canterbury proposed, as 'faith seeking understanding', Bede surely qualifies in the theological line alone. If the definition can be expanded to include those who exercise their minds with great intellectual power upon the many aspects of the work of God, then this was Bede's life's work and in every sphere about which he wrote he made a lasting contribution to Christian understanding.

In language, for instance, Bede gave an enormous impetus in his own times to the learning of Latin in England and also to the use of the vernacular by translation and by composition in Anglo-Saxon prose and poetry, but more important than this is the beautiful Latin of his works, providing a permanent collection of fine Latin prose for posterity. With regard to his work in calculating time, he gave shape to our times, by establishing the present AD dating and popularizing it throughout Europe, something so taken for granted that its brilliance is seldom noticed. For instruction in the calculation of time, Bede was the master of the Middle Ages; his treatises were known, used and copied for centuries in any monastery concerned with instruction in astronomy, while his paschal tables were indispensable for the computation of the ecclesiastical calendar. In natural science, alone in his age, he selected from the material available to him with a clear and workable method, providing a respectable body of material from which he drew some inferences that were unparalleled in his time, advancing studies to a point which made them authorities throughout the West until the seventeenth century.

As an historian, he used and improved the pattern of the seven ages of the world, providing a scheme for thinking about world history, always with the eighth age of the eternity of God in his mind as the perspective of reality. The book for which he is best known today, the *Ecclesiastical History*, still provides early documents, contemporary comment, and a link with the past which is fresh, vivid and available. His historical method was so sophisticated that it is often paid the compliment of criticism as if it had emerged in the nineteenth century. It is, however, worth remembering that Bede's historical writings were for him and for his contemporaries a part of Christian rhetoric, to help save souls by warning and encouragement. For a modern historian they still hold a central place, but for quite different reasons: they are works to be mined for information about the past as well as providing a pattern of historical method by a master. The fact that his information is still sound says much for Bede the historian, but the gaps which modern investigators find in his pages are often not a sign of weakness in him but of a different interest and purpose. The popularity of the *Ecclesiastical History* has continued unabated and still provides the greatest amount of what is known about the early history of the English, and that is unique; no other historian of the barbarians did the same. The concept of 'Englishness' is also one formed by Bede in his *History*, for his phrase *gens anglorum* was new. But this was in no sense an exclusive nationalism; Bede saw the English as a *gens*, a tribe, a part of the people of God, of the Church in heaven and on earth, and all that was dear to him in his own experience and in his love of the past of his race was transmuted into a wider ethos.

In the area of directly 'ecclesiastical' writing, Bede preserved many accounts of the saints and organized their veneration in a martyrology which formed the basis of every subsequent revision. But his saints did not become merely formalized hierarchic figures; they remain human and familiar. Hilda, Caedmon, Chad, Aidan, Oswald would be unknown except for Bede, and they live in stories he recounted in a way uniquely attractive.

Least read of Bede's works are those he placed first in his own list of his writings and for which he was best known in his own day, his biblical commentaries. These contain the main part of his theological work. It is often said they need to be looked at either in order to see what he transmitted of the early Latin patristic tradition or in order to understand better his work as an historian. This is so, but that was not why they were either written or valued originally. Bede continued the patristic tradition of commentary on the Bible with his own work, offering a clear and thorough elucidation of the Scriptures, turning the word of God into a vehicle for prayer and conversion of life for his contemporaries, and they became as invaluable for preachers commenting on Scripture as for monks meditating upon it. In the twelfth century, a large amount from his commentaries was incorporated into the textbook of the time, the *Glossa Ordinaria*: for commentary on Ezra and Nehemiah, Tobit, Proverbs and Habakkuk he was the sole authority cited, and passages were included in the *Glossa* along with sections from Augustine, Jerome, Ambrose and Gregory from almost all of the books for which he had provided a commentary. His work was used by the friars, both in the *Catena Aurea* of Thomas Aquinas and in the works of the Franciscan Bonaventura. His commentaries and homilies have continued in use in the Office for reading at Vigils.[26] Recent critical editions and translations of Bede's biblical commentaries make these more accessible and it may be that after so many years in this century in which scriptural study has been dominated by an utterly different approach, such commentaries may again have their original usefulness.

Bede was both loved and valued in his own times and is so today, though not always for the same reasons. The only English Doctor of the Church and the most learned man of his age, Bede's work cannot be separated from himself. After twelve centuries it is a remarkable fact that one about whose life so little is known still seems a friend and contemporary. The character of Bede himself, always discreet and self-effacing, inspires love and a sense of familiarity still:

> [Bede's] gifts and habits were those of a scholar. His capacious mind was seldom swayed by prejudice, firm in its judgments, well fitted to deal with a large mass of disorderly material and to present it systematically and succinctly. Like many men of this stamp, he never obtrudes his own personality, seldom mentions his own experience, keeps his eye steadily on the material before him, and expresses his condemnation more often by silence than by strictures. His piety was exact and unwavering, his diligence unremitting. His last hours, spent in translating the Bible and abbreviating a learned work among his friends, breaking out at one moment unexpectedly into the poetic idiom of his ancestors, perfectly reflect the range of his activity and the unruffled temper of his life and death.[27]

It is because of this steady unity between thought and action that Bede's writings still prove accessible beyond those of other men:

> There is no period in the history of Britain or of the English Church in which Bede is antiquated; in every generation he speaks familiarly.[28]

In the liturgy of the Church, the feast of Bede was until recently celebrated on the day after his death, 27 May, but has now been moved to 25 May. A collect for his Mass runs:

> O God, who dost illuminate thy Church with the learning of blessed Bede thy confessor and doctor: graciously grant unto thy servants that they may ever be enlightened by his wisdom and aided by his merits.

More moving to those who still find him a master and a friend is a visit to the site of the foundations of the monastic cells at Jarrow, where visitors were shown in the eleventh century, still standing after the Viking attacks and the desolation of the North, a little house of stone, in which it was his custom to sit, away from all that could disturb him, to reflect and read, to dictate and to write.[29]

Notes

1 Bull of Leo XIII, *Urbi et Orbi: Acta Sanctae Sedis in compendium opportune redacta et illustrata*, ed. V. Piazzesi, XXXII (Rome, 1900), pp. 338–9. Cf. also Benedict XIV, *De servorum dei beatificatione et beatorum canonizatione* (Bologna, 1738), IV, 2, 12, 9, indicating that approval for the celebration of an Office and the Mass *O doctor optime*, granted in honour of Bede, constituted canonization as a Doctor of the Church.

2 *Letter of Cuthbert*, p. 583.

3 Eadmer, *The Life of St Anselm, Archbishop of Canterbury*, ed. and trans. R. W. Southern (London, 1962), II.lxvi, pp. 141–3.

4 *Letter of Cuthbert on the Death of Bede*, HE, p. 582; the quotation is from Paulinus, *Life of St Ambrose* (PL 14, 43).

5 *Letters of Cuthbert*, ed. M. Tangl, *Monumenta Germaniae Historica: Epistolae selectae* I (Berlin, 1916; hereafter referred to as Tangl), *Letter* 116, pp. 250–2.

6 Alcuin, *The Bishops, Kings and Saints of York*, ed. and trans. P. Godman (Oxford, 1983) II, 1315–1318, pp. 103–5.

7 *Letter of Cuthbert*, Tangl 116, p. 250.

8 *The Letters of Saint Boniface*, trans. E. Emerton (Columbia University, New York, 1940), *Letter* LIX, p. 133.

9 Ibid., *Letter* LX, p. 134.

10 Ibid., *Letter* LXXV, p. 168.

11 *Letter of Cuthbert*, Tangl 116, p. 252.

12 *Luke*, Prologue, p. 7.

13 *Letter of Lul*, Tangl 125; trans. in M. Parkes (see below, note 14), p. 15.

14 Cf. M. Parkes, *The Scriptorium of Wearmouth–Jarrow* (Jarrow Lecture, 1982), p. 32.

15 *Alcuin of York, his Life and Letters*, ed. S. Allott (York, 1974), *Letter* 29, p. 40.

16 Alcuin, *The Bishops, Kings and Saints of York*, pp. 103–5.

17 Cf. Francis Wormald, *English Kalendars before 1100* (London, 1934).

18 William of Malmesbury, *Vita S. Wulstani*, ed. R. R. Darlington, Camden 3rd Series 40 (London, 1928), I. 14, p. 20.

19 *History of the Church of Durham*, ed. T. Arnold, Rolls Series 18 (London, 1882), I. 14, p. 42; trans. J. Stephenson (1858). Attributed to Symeon of Durham; I follow A. Grandsen in thinking this doubtful: cf. A. Grandsen, *Historical Writing in England, c. 550 to c. 1307* (London, 1974; 1982), p. 116.

20 *History of the Church of Durham*, III.7, pp. 87–9.

21 For an account of the return of monks to Jarrow and their transference to Durham, see ibid., II. 189ff. Discussed by A. J. Piper, *The Durham Monks at Jarrow* (Jarrow Lecture, 1986).

22 Cf. Bede's *Commentary on Revelation* 2:28, col. 140 (Marshall, p. 32).

23 Amalarius of Metz, *De Ecclesiasticis Officiis* (PL 105, 1164C).

24 Thomas Aquinas, *Summa Theologiae* Ia, 65–74, Blackfriars edn, 10:

Cosmogony, ed. and trans. William A. Wallace OP (Oxford, 1966), appendix 8, pp. 211–18, for his opinion of Bede's DNR; he also used Bede's homilies and commentaries extensively in the *Catena Aurea*.

25 Robert Bellarmine, *Opera Omnia*, ed. Sforza (Naples, 1872), p. 63, quoted in the Bull of Pope Leo XIII, op. cit. (note 1 above).

26 For a list of the selections from Bede used at Matins in the Roman Breviary (pre-1980) see M. I. Carroll, *The Venerable Bede: his Spiritual Teachings* (Washington, DC, 1946), pp. 65–6.

27 R. W. Southern, 'Bede' in *Medieval Humanism* (New York, 1970), pp. 1–8.

28 W. P. Ker, *The Dark Ages* (London, 1904), p. 141.

29 *History of the Church of Durham*, 15, p. 646.

Abbreviations and Bibliography

PL   *Patrologia Latina*, ed. J. P. Migne (221 vols, Paris, 1844–64). Numbers refer to PL columns, not pages.
CCSL   *Corpus Christianorum, Series Latina* (Turnhout).
Giles   *Venerabilis Bedae opera quae supersunt omnia*, ed. J. A. Giles (12 vols, London, 1843–44).
BLTW   *Bede: Life, Times and Writings*, ed. A. H. Thompson (Oxford, 1935).
Famulus Christi   *Famulus Christi*, ed. G. Bonner (London, 1976).

Quotations from the Bible are from the Authorized Version; psalms are numbered according to the Vulgate with the numbers for the Book of Common Prayer in brackets.

Bede's works

Historical works

HE   *Ecclesiastical History of the English People*, ed. and trans. B. Colgrave and R. A. B. Mynors (Oxford, 1969).
HE(P)   *Bedae Historia Ecclesiastica Gentis Anglorum: Venerabilis Bedae opera historica*, ed. C. Plummer (2 vols, Oxford, 1896).
HA   *History of the Abbots of Wearmouth and Jarrow*, ed. C. Plummer in HE(P) I, pp. 364–87.
HA (Farmer)   Trans. in *The Age of Bede*, ed. D. Farmer (Harmondsworth, 1965; 1985), pp. 185–208.

Chronica Minora, Chronica Maiora   Edited separately from the treatises *De Temporibus* and *De Temporum Ratione* (see below) of which they formed part by T. Mommsen in *Monumenta*

Germaniae Historica: Auctores antiquissimi XIII (Berlin, 1898), pp. 231–327.
Also in DT, pp. 585–611 and DTR, pp. 463–544 (see below).

Letter to Egbert   Ed. C. Plummer in HE(P) I, pp. 405–23.
Letter to Egbert (Whitelock)   Trans. D. Whitelock in *English Historical Documents* 1: *500–1042*, no. 170 (London, 1955).
Letter of Cuthbert   Epistola de obitu Bedae, text and trans. B. Colgrave and R. A. B. Mynors, HE, pp. 580–6.
   Giles I, pp. clxiiiff.

Hagiography

VSC   *Vita Sancti Cuthberti Prosaica*, ed. and trans. B. Colgrave in *Two Lives of St Cuthbert* (Cambridge, 1940).
VSC(Met)   *Vita Sancti Cuthberti Metrica*, critical edition: *Bedas metrische Vita Sancti Cuthberti*, ed. W. Jaeger (Leipzig, 1935).
   PL 94, 575–93.
   Giles I, pp. 1–35.

Felix   Vita S. Felicis
   PL 94, 789–97.
   Giles IV, pp. 174–202.

Martryrology   Kalendarium sive Martyrologia, ed. C. W. Jones, CCSL CXXIIIC (Turnhout, 1980), pp. 567–78.

Didactic works

DO   *De Orthographia*, ed. C. W. Jones, *Bedae opera didascalica*, CCSL CXXIIIA (Turnhout, 1975), pp. 7–57.
DAM   *De Arte Metrica*, ed. C. W. Jones, CCSL CXXIIIA, pp. 82–141.
DST   *De Schematibus et Tropis*, ed. C. W. Jones, CCSL CXXIIIA, pp. 142–71.
DT   *Liber de Temporibus*, ed. C. W. Jones, *Bedae Opera De Temporibus* (Medieval Academy of America, Cambridge, Massachusetts, 1943).
   Also (with *Chronica Minora*) in CCSL CXXIIIC, pp. 585–611.
DTR   *De Temporum Ratione*, ed. C. W. Jones (with *Chronica Maiora*), CCSL CXXIIIB (Turnhout, 1978), pp. 263–460.
DNR   *Liber de Natura Rerum*, ed. C. W. Jones, CCSL CXXIIIA, pp. 190–235.

ABBREVIATIONS AND BIBLIOGRAPHY

Biblical works

Samuel   In Primam Partem Samuhelis Libri IIII, ed. D. Hurst, CCSL CXIX (Turnhout, 1969).

Questions   In Regum Librum XXX Questiones, ed. D. Hurst, CCSL CXIX, pp. 293–322.

Genesis   Libri Quatuor In Principium Genesis, ed. C. W. Jones, CCSL CXVIII (Turnhout, 1967).

Tabernacle   De Tabernaculo et Vasis eius ac Vestibus Sacerdotum, ed. D. Hurst, CCSL CXIX, pp. 5–139.

Temple   De Templo, ed. D. Hurst, CCSL CXIX, pp. 143–234.

Ezra   In Ezram et Neemiam, ed. D. Hurst, CCSL CXIX, pp. 237–392.

Tobit   In Librum Patris Tobiae Allegorica Expositio, ed. D. Hurst, CCSL CXIXB (Turnhout, 1983), pp. 3–19.

Proverbs   In Proverbia Salomonis, ed. D. Hurst, CCSL CXIXB, pp. 23–136.

Song of Songs   In Cantica Canticorum Allegorica Expositio, ed. D. Hurst, CCSL CXIXB, pp. 167–375.

Habakkuk   In Canticum Habacuc Allegorica Expositio, ed. J. E. Hudson, CCSL CXIXB, pp. 381–409.

Acts/Acts(R)   Expositio Actuum Apostolorum et Retractio, ed. M. L. W. Laistner, Medieval Academy of America Publication no. 35 (Cambridge, Massachusetts, 1939).
    Also in CCSL CXXI (Turnhout, 1983), pp. 3–163.

Luke   In Lucae Evangelium Expositio, ed. D. Hurst, CCSL CXX (Turnhout, 1960), pp. 5–425.

Mark   In Marci Evangelium Expositio, ed. D. Hurst, CCSL CXX, pp. 43–648.

Epistles   Super Epistulas Catholicas Expositio, ed. D. Hurst, CCSL CXXI.

Epistles (Hurst)   Trans. D. Hurst, *On the Seven Catholic Epistles* (Kalamazoo, Michigan, 1985).

Revelation   PL 93, 129–207.
    Giles XII, pp. 337–452.

Revelation (Marshall)   Partial trans. E. Marshall, *The Explanation of the Apocalypse by Venerable Beda* (Oxford, 1878).

Other works

Homilies   Opera Homilectica, ed. D. Hurst, CCSL CXXII (Turnhout, 1955), pp. 1–378.

Poems   Liber Hymnorum Rhythmi Variae Preces, ed. J. Fraipont, CCSL CXXII, pp. 407–70.

151

Bibliography

Anglo-Saxon England, ed. J. Campbell, E. John and P. Wormald (1987).

Anglo-Saxon Northumbria, ed. M. Lapidge and P. Hunter Blair (London, 1984).

Bede and His World (Jarrow Lectures; 2 vols; London, 1994).

Bede: Life, Times and Writings, ed. A. H. Thompson (Oxford, 1935).

P. Hunter Blair, *Northumbria in the Days of Bede* (London, 1966).

P. Hunter Blair, *The World of Bede* (London, 1970).

G. Bonner, *Saint Bede in the Tradition of Western Apocalyptic Commentary* (Jarrow Lecture, 1966).

G. Bonner, 'The Christian life in the thought of the Venerable Bede', *Durham University Journal* LXII (1970).

G. Bonner, 'Bede and medieval civilization', *Anglo-Saxon England* 11 (1973), pp. 71–90.

G. Bonner, 'The saints of Durham', *Sobornost*, new series, 8 (1986).

G. Bonner, 'Bede and his legacy', *Durham University Journal* LXXVIII.2 (June 1986).

R. L. S. Bruce-Mitford, *The Sutton Hoo Ship-Burial: A Handbook* (London, 1976).

J. Campbell, 'Bede' in *Latin Historians*, ed. T. A. Dorey (London, 1966).

James Campbell, *Essays in Anglo-Saxon History* (London, 1986).

B. Capelle, 'Le rôle théologique de Bède le Vénérable', *Studia Anselmiana* VI (1936), pp. 1–40.

M. T. A. Carroll, *The Venerable Bede and his Spiritual Teachings* (Washington, DC, 1946).

R. W. Chambers, 'Bede', *Proceedings of the British Academy* 32 (1936), pp. 3–30.

T. M. Charles-Edwards, 'Bede, the Irish and the Britons', *Celtica* 5 (1983), pp. 42–52.

H. E. J. Cowdrey, 'Bede and the English people', *Journal of Religious History* 11 (1981), pp. 501–23.

R. H. C. Davis and J. M. Wallace-Hadrill, *The Writing of History in the Middle Ages: Essays Presented to R. W. Southern* (Oxford, 1981).

Henri de Lubac SJ, *Exégèse Médiévale: les quatre sens de l'Ecriture* (4 vols; Paris, 1959).

I. M. Douglas, 'Bede *De Templo* and the Commentary on Samuel and Kings by Claudius of Turin' in *Famulus Christi*, pp. 325–34.

T. B. Ekenrode, 'The Venerable Bede as scientist', *American Benedictine Review* XXI (1971), pp. 496–507.

Famulus Christi: Essays in Commemoration of the Thirteenth Centenary of the Birth of the Venerable Bede, ed. G. Bonner (London, 1976).

V. I. J. Flint, 'The true author of the *Salonii Commentarii in Parabolas et in Ecclesiasten*', *Recherches de théologie ancienne et médiévale* 37 (1970), pp. 174–86.

P. Geary, *Furta Sacra: Theft of Relics in the Central Middle Ages* (Princeton, NJ, 1978).

C. Jenkins, 'Bede as exegete and theologian' in BLTW, pp. 152–201.

E. John, *Orbis Britanniae* (Leicester, 1966).

C. W. Jones, *Bedae Opera De Temporibus* (Cambridge, MA, 1943).

C. W. Jones, *Saints' Lives and Chronicles* (Ithaca, NY, 1947).

D. Knowles, 'Bede the Venerable' in *Saints and Scholars: Twenty Five Medieval Portraits* (Cambridge, 1961).

M. Laistner, 'Source marks in Bede manuscripts', *Journal of Theological Studies* 31 (1933), pp. 350–4.

M. L. Laistner, *A Handlist of Bede Manuscripts* (New York, 1943).

M. L. Laistner, *Thought and Letters in Western Europe* (2nd edn; London, 1957).

H. E. Loyn, *Anglo-Saxon England and the Norman Conquest* (London, 1962).

J. McClure, 'Bede's Old Testament Kings' in *Ideal and Reality in Frankish and Anglo-Saxon Society*, ed. P. Wormald, D. Bullough and R. Collins (Oxford, 1983), pp. 76–99.

J. McClure, 'Bede's *Notes on Genesis* and the training of the Anglo-Saxon clergy' in *The Bible in the Medieval World*, ed. K. Walsh and D. Wood (Oxford, 1985).

R. A. Markus, *Bede and the Tradition of Ecclesiastical Historiography* (Jarrow Lecture, 1975).

H. M. R. E. Mayr-Harting, *The Coming of Christianity to Anglo-Saxon England* (London, 1972).

Paul Meyvaert, *Bede and Gregory the Great* (Jarrow Lecture, 1964).

Paul Meyvaert, 'Bede the scholar', in *Famulus Christi*, pp. 40–70.

Paul Meyvaert, *Benedict, Gregory, Bede and Others* (London, 1977).

M. Parkes, *The Scriptorium of Wearmouth–Jarrow* (Jarrow Lecture, 1982).

A. J. Piper, *The Durham Monks at Jarrow* (Jarrow Lecture, 1986).

C. Plummer, *Baedae Opera Historica* (2 vols, Oxford, 1896; vol. 1, preface; vol. 2, notes).

R. L. Poole, *Chronicles and Annals* (Oxford, 1926).

R. L. Poole, *Studies in Chronology and History* (Oxford, 1934).

J. O. Prestwich, 'King Aethelhere and the Battle of the Winwaed', *English Historical Review* 83 (1968), pp. 89–95.

D. Rollason, *Saints and Relics in Anglo-Saxon England* (Oxford, 1989).

R. W. Southern, 'Bede' in *Medieval Humanism* (New York, 1970), pp. 1–9.

A. Stacpoole OSB, 'St Bede' in *Benedict's Disciples*, ed. D. H. Farmer (Leominster, 1980), pp. 86–105.

F. Stenton, *Anglo-Saxon England* (3rd edn; Oxford, 1971).

Wesley M. Stevens, *Bede's Scientific Achievments* (Jarrow Lecture, 1985).

A. Thacker, 'Bede's ideal of reform' in *Ideal and Reality in Frankish and Anglo-Saxon Society*, ed. P. Wormald, D. Bullough and R. Collins (Oxford, 1983).

M. Wallace-Hadrill, *Bede's Europe* (Jarrow Lecture, 1962).

M. Wallace-Hadrill, *Early Germanic Kingship in England and on the Continent* (Oxford, 1971).

M. Wallace-Hadrill, *Bede's Ecclesiastical History: An Historical Commentary* (Oxford, 1988). (This includes a valuable bibliography of the massive secondary literature surrounding the *Ecclesiastical History*.)

B. Ward, 'Bede and the conversion of the Anglo-Saxons' in *St Bede: A Tribute (735–1985)* (Massachusetts, 1985), pp. 34–47.

B. Ward, *Bede and the Psalter* (Jarrow Lecture, 1991).

D. Whitelock, *After Bede* (Jarrow Lecture, 1960).

D. Whitelock, 'Bede and his teachers and friends' in *Famulus Christi*, pp. 19–40.

D. Wilson (ed.), *The Archaeology of Anglo-Saxon England* (London, 1976).

Index

Acca, Bp of Hexham 5, 12, 51, 56, 58, 61, 67–8, 80
Adamnan 59, 125
Aebbe, Abbess 125
Aethelberht, King 15, 108, 117–19
Aethelburgh, Queen 16, 104, 119
Aethelfrith, King 118
Aethelthryth, Queen 13, 24, 37, 95, 103, 125, 126
Aidan 11, 16, 38, 100–1, 104, 107–8, 114, 122
Alban 100
Albinus, Abbot 7
Alcuin 9, 138
Aldfrith, King 127, 130
Aldhelm of Malmesbury 8, 25
Ambrose 8, 26, 51, 60, 68–9, 95, 135
Augustine of Canterbury 15, 117–18
Augustine of Hippo 7, 20, 26, 47, 54, 60, 68, 74, 95

Bamburgh 104
Bede
  works: *Chronica Maiora* 131–2; *Chronica Minora* 131–2; *Commentary on the Book of Proverbs* 75; *Commentary on the Book of Tobit* 74; *Commentary on the Canticle of Habakkuk* 77–8; *Commentary on Ezra and Nehemiah* 72–4; *Commentary on Genesis* 68–72; *Commentary on Samuel* 4, 67–8; *Commentary on the Song of Songs* 6, 75–7; *De Natura Rerum* 13, 34, 36; *De Orthographica* 22; *De*

Schematis et Tropis 23; *De Temporibus* 27, 33; *De Temporum Ratione* 3, 11, 27, 33, 34, 51, 72, 114; *Ecclesiastical History of the English People* 114–29; 3, 12, 16, 23, 26, 28, 35, 38, 56, 59, 66, 72, 77, 79, 80–1, 88, 90, 93, 96–7, 99, 101, 103, 106, 108, 111–12, 130, 138, 144–5; *History of the Abbots of Wearmouth and Jarrow* 3, 4, 14, 88, 93, 96, 106; *Letter to Egbert* 37, 78, 81, 129–31; *Liber Retractationis* 13, 59; *Life of St Anastasius* 97; *Life of St Cuthbert* 6, 11, 97, 98, 138; *Life of St Felix* 97
  life: own account 2; early life 4; as pupil 6–8; as teacher 19–39; as biblical scholar 41–84; as hagiographer 88–108; mocked by his brethren 14; accused of heresy 57; death 134–5
  sources for his writings 8, 22, 42, 43–7, 50–2, 60, 64, 67–8, 75
  cult: early veneration 136–9; in England 139–43
Benedict Biscop 2, 5–8, 16, 37–8, 42, 45, 62, 83, 106–7, 124, 135
Benedict of Nursia 9, 96
Bertha, Queen 108, 119
Boisil 21, 128
Boniface, Bp 136

Caedmon 26, 108
Caelin 108

155